PAS DE PANIQUE!

PAS DE PANIQUE!

A Basic French Course for GCSE

David Edwards

Nelson

The author would like to thank the following people for their help:

Elisabeth Normand, Patrice Vérien, Micheline Normand, Yvonne Matthews, Léon Rotureau, Guy Brytygier, le Collège Lucien Millet à Doué-la-Fontaine.

Thomas Nelson and Sons Ltd
Nelson House   Mayfield Road
Walton-on-Thames   Surrey
KT12 5PL   UK

58 Albany Street
Edinburgh
EH1 3QR   UK

Thomas Nelson (Hong Kong) Ltd
Toppan Building 10/F
22A Westlands Road
Quarry Bay   Hong Kong

Thomas Nelson Australia
102 Dodds Street
South Melbourne
Victoria 3205   Australia

Nelson Canada
1120 Birchmount Road
Scarborough   Ontario
M1K 5G4   Canada

First published by Macmillan Education Ltd 1988
ISBN 0-333-46223-8

This edition published by Thomas Nelson and Sons Ltd 1991

ISBN 0-17-439711-9
NPN 9 8 7 6 5 4 3

Printed in China.

Table des matières

To the student

With your teacher's help, this book should do three important things for you:

1 It will teach or remind you of the French you need to get by in France.
2 It will tell you something about France and the French, and show you some of the interesting differences between our and their ways of organising things.
3 It will help prepare you for the Basic Level of the GCSE examination.

Remember that the important thing is for you to have a go at speaking French and getting your meaning across. You can make mistakes in French without that stopping a French person from understanding you.

Don't forget that you can look up any word in the vocabulary list at the back of the book.

The following symbols tell you what sort of task you are being asked to attempt. You can often also use the French in them when you are speaking to someone.

Symbol	Meaning	You should…
j'apprends	I'm learning	memorise something
je cherche	I'm searching	look for information
j'écoute	I'm listening	listen carefully
j'écris	I'm writing	write
je travaille	I'm working	carry out a task
je lis	I'm reading	read and understand
je parle	I'm speaking	speak with your partner
je révise je révise je révise	I'm revising	revise
DIRECTIONS	signs	learn these useful signs
trois... deux... un...TOP!	countdown	answer the taped questions before the bleep

To the teacher

Teachers may make copies of the following blank chart for students to use with each listening exercise. Copy the column headings from the printed listening charts into the blank space at the top of this chart. Then, as students listen to the tape, they can fill in their answers in the appropriate columns of their charts.

1	
2	
3	
4	
5	
6	
7	
8	
9	
10	

Meeting people and chatting to them

When you meet French people you will probably find that they want to know all kinds of things about you: your name, your age, where you live, how big a place it is and so on. It's a good idea to have a few answers ready and also to be able to ask them the same sort of questions.

We will look at how to ask and answer the basic questions and also a few you may not know.

When you first meet someone…

…in England you might say 'hello', or 'how do you do?' if it is a more formal meeting. In France it is more or less the same:

bonjour!	hello
enchanté!	how do you do?

Ces garçons se rencontrent après une journée au collège.
Certains possèdent un vélo; d'autres ont une mobylette.
En France: si tu as quatorze ans, tu peux rouler à mobylette.

> *le vélo* – bicycle
> *le vélomoteur* – moped
> *rouler* – ride/drive
> *se rencontrent* – meet

Here are a few phrases which you need to know when you meet someone:

ça va?	how are you?
comment ça va?	how are you?
bonjour!	hello!
salut!	(Curiously enough, this word can be used to mean either 'hello' or 'goodbye' when you're talking to friends.)

Ces filles se rencontrent dans la cour du collège.
Elles ont un cartable.

> *la cour* – playground
> *le cartable* – schoolbag

A *j'écoute* Listen to the tape. You'll hear ten sets of people being introduced to one another, or meeting for the first time. As you hear each dialogue, listen out for the words or phrases which you've been reminded about so far and tick them off on your copy of this chart. Don't let the speed of the French worry you, and ignore anything that gets in the way of your spotting the information you're looking for.

	Bonjour!	*Salut!*	*Ça va ?*	*Comment ça va?*	*Enchanté!*
1					
2					
3					
4					
5					

Did you know…?

In France they shake hands much more often than we do, not only when they meet someone for the first time, but also every time they meet them after that!
If your French friend has a lot of other friends, you could end up with a sore hand!

?!

je révise
je révise
je révise

Do you recognise these questions? You may find it easier if your teacher reads them to you:

Comment t'appelles-tu?
Quel âge as-tu?
Est-ce que tu as des frères ou des soeurs?
Comment s'appelle ton frère?
Comment s'appelle ta soeur?
Qu'est-ce qu'il fait dans la vie, ton père?
Qu'est-ce qu'elle fait dans la vie, ta mère?

You need to be able **both** to ask and to answer these questions because then you'll be able to start a conversation with someone you've just met.

Here is how to begin your answers to the questions:

Je m'appelle ……	(name)
J'ai …… ans	(age)
J'ai …… frère(s)/soeur(s)	(brother(s)/sister(s))
Mon frère s'appelle ……	(name of brother)
Ma soeur s'appelle ……	(name of sister)
Mon père est……	(Dad's job)
Ma mère est ……	(Mum's job)

If you're an only child, or you're not sure how to say what your mum or dad do for a living, ask your teacher what to say.

Here are some typical jobs:

fermier/fermière	farmer	*facteur*	postman
secrétaire	secretary	*employé(e) de banque*	bank clerk
infirmier/infirmière	nurse	*routier/une femme routier*	lorry driver
coiffeur/coiffeuse	hairdresser	*professeur*	teacher
maçon/une femme maçon	builder	*ménagère*	housewife
chômeur/chômeuse	unemployed		

je parle

With your partner, practise asking and answering the questions we've been looking at.

Work in pairs. One of you should look at **this** page and the other at page 159.

For this game, you are a frontier police-officer looking for a jewel thief. The false identity she or he is likely to use appears below. But **be careful!** Time is short, and innocent tourists can't be kept waiting! You may ask **four** questions, but then you must move on to another tourist (your partner plays the part of **all** the tourists!). Your partner will try to get her or his thief through your checkpoint…! Don't forget that an innocent tourist may just have the same name as the jewel thief. You lose if you challenge an innocent tourist! When you make the arrest, say *'je vous arrête'*. Don't get it wrong or you could get dragged through the courts!

The thief

Noms utilisés par le voleur: Dupont, Dumeil, Durand, LeBlanc, Dutheil
Âge du voleur: 32 ans
Composition de sa famille: 1 frère (Jean), 1 soeur (Marie)
Profession des parents: son père est banquier et sa mère est informaticienne

  informaticienne – computer technician

Listen carefully to what Robert says he likes or dislikes. All the things he mentions are shown on this page. On your copy of this chart, put a tick in the appropriate column to show what he likes and dislikes.

J'aime
Je n'aime pas

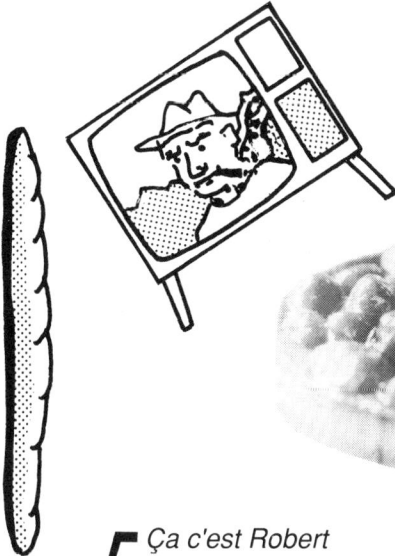

Ça c'est Robert

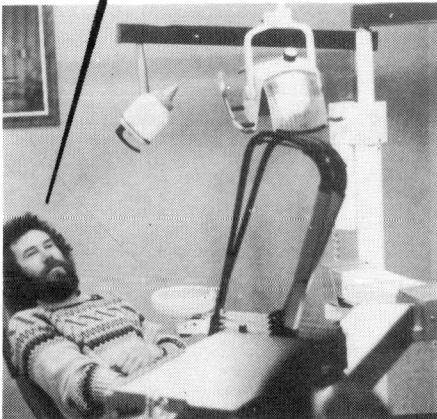

		likes	dislikes
1	snails		
2	the dentist		
3	Westerns		
4	fresh bread		
5	playing the guitar		
6	listening to cassettes		
7	fruit tarts		

Où est-ce qu'on se donne rendez-vous?

Something you will need to be able to do when you are in France is to arrange a meeting.

There are usually **three** parts to this operation:

1 arranging the day (it could be today);
2 arranging the time;
3 arranging the place.

Have a look at the examples.

*On se donne rendez-vous
vendredi
à sept heures et quart
devant la piscine*

*On se donne rendez-vous
mardi
à quatre heures
devant le collège*

Check that you
remember the
days of the week.

dimanche · lundi · mardi · mercredi · jeudi · vendredi · samedi

la semaine

je révise
je révise
je révise

Quelle heure est-il, s'il vous plaît?

a

b

c

d

e

f

g

h

i

j

k

l

Check:

1 that you still know how to ask what time it is;
2 that you can tell the time in all the cases above (a to l).

à   This is used to mean 'at' as in *à une heure* (at one o'clock).

1 *On se donne rendez-vous à huit heures en face du collège.*
2 *On se donne rendez-vous à deux heures et quart près de l'église.*
3 *On se donne rendez-vous à trois heures et demie en face du supermarché.*
4 *On se donne rendez-vous à six heures moins le quart à côté du garage.*
5 *On se donne rendez-vous à sept heures vingt-cinq derrière le cinéma.*

je parle   With your partner, practise telling the time by drawing clock faces onto a scrap of paper (or into your exercise book, if your teacher agrees) and asking each other:

Quelle heure est-il, s'il vous plaît?

On se donne rendez-vous...

On se donne rendez-vous	lundi mardi mercredi jeudi vendredi samedi dimanche	à	une heure deux heures (etc.)	en face près à côté	du collège. de la banque. du cinéma. du stade de l'hôtel. de la mairie. (etc.)

Your teacher will show you how to use this block diagram to build your own sentences and set up meetings. Don't go on until you are sure you understand.

You may have noticed that expressions like *près de*, *en face de*, *à côté de* and so on change a little according to what is after them, whereas *devant* and *derrière* do not. The next table shows this.

en face près à côté	du collège
devant derrière	le collège

opposite near next to	the school
in front of behind	the school

*On se donne rendez-vous lundi à deux heures près **du collège**.*
*On se donne rendez-vous lundi à deux heures près **de la gare**.*

Don't worry if you keep getting this wrong, you will still be understood. If you do want to get it right though, notice whether the various places are **un** words or **une** words.
In the two sentences given above for example:

> *collège* is an **un** word – **un** *collège*
> *gare* is an **une** word – **une** *gare*

Try to suggest other places to meet, using words like *près de*, etc. with some of the place names which you will find on page 56.

je travaille   Can you decide what should go in the gaps here? Read them aloud filling in the blanks:

1   *On se donne rendez-vous mardi à huit heures à côté ...... banque.*
2   *On se donne rendez-vous vendredi à deux heures près .... collège.*
3   *On se donne rendez-vous mardi à six heures en face ...... discothèque.*
    (*discothèque* is an **une** word)
4   *On se donne rendez-vous samedi à deux heures et demie près ......gare.*
5   *On se donne rendez-vous mercredi à une heure à côté...... patinoire.*
    (*patinoire* is an **une** word and means skating rink)

Les dates

When you want to arrange a meeting with someone on a particular date begin as usual with:

1 **On se donne rendez-vous**

2 ... add the word **le**

3 ... add the number **vingt-cinq**

4 ... add the month **mai...**

Les mois de l'année

janvier	juillet
février	août
mars	septembre
avril	octobre
mai	novembre
juin	décembre

C
j'écoute

Listen to these ten sets of people arranging meetings.

Using your copy of this chart, in the first box, try to write what the people are going to **do**, then try to write the **date**, **time** and **place** of each meeting. Of course, they may well meet in **one** place to go to **another**.

	activity	day or date	time	place
1				
2				
3				

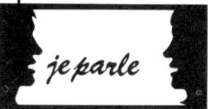

je parle

With your partner, arrange meetings using the details below. Either of you may need to ask for some detail that your partner has not given you. You may find these questions handy: *à quelle heure?* (at what time?), *quel jour?* (on what day or date?) *où ça?* (whereabouts?).

1	Tuesday	at 3.00 pm	in front of the garage
2	Wednesday	at 1.00 pm	opposite the school
3	Friday	at 4.00 pm	next to the sweet shop
4	Sunday	at 6.00 pm	outside the cinema
5	Monday	at 7.15 pm	opposite the town hall
6	21st July	at 5.00 pm	at the theatre
7	3rd August	at 4.30 pm	near the pool
8	2nd September	at 2.00 pm	opposite the bank
9	5th May	at 3.00 pm	in front of the theatre
10	16th September	at 6.15 pm	outside the station

(Don't forget the vocabulary at the back of the book if you're stuck!)

Bonjour! Ça va?

Dialogue 1

Jean	Tu veux bien aller à la disco?
Marie	Oui... mais quand?
Jean	Mardi... on se donne rendez-vous à sept heures et demie en face de la disco, d'accord?
Marie	Mardi... à sept heures et demie en face de la disco. D'accord.

Dialogue 2

Hélène	On va à la piscine?
Claire	Oui, bonne idée. On y va quand?
Hélène	Ce soir?
Claire	D'accord... où est-ce qu'on se donne rendez-vous?
Hélène	Eh bien, devant la piscine, ce soir à six heures.

Dialogue 3

Pierre	Quand est-ce qu'on va au cinéma?
Anne	Vendredi... on se donne rendez-vous derrière la gare routière à cinq heures et quart, d'accord?
Pierre	D'accord.

Dialogue 4

Jean	Tu voudrais aller au restaurant?
Marie-Claire	Quand ça?
Jean	Eh bien... demain soir.
Marie-Claire	Je veux bien... quand est-ce qu'on se donne rendez-vous?
Jean	À sept heures et quart devant la mairie.

La tour Eiffel

This sign means that you have to read what follows and get the gist of it! You don't need to be able to understand every word.

Voici la tour Eiffel.

Trois cent travailleurs ont construit la tour entre 1887 et 1889.

La tour a 320,75 mètres de hauteur. Elle a 2500000 rivets et elle pèse 7000 tonnes.

Tous les sept ans, on peint la tour. On utilise 52 tonnes de peinture!

la hauteur – height
on utilise – they use

Voici la Seine.

C'est un fleuve.
Sur la rive droite il y a un bâtiment
circulaire. C'est la maison de la
radio et de la télévision.

Près de la rive gauche il y a des
péniches.

> un fleuve – a river
> une rive – a bank (of a river)
> un bâtiment – a building
> une péniche – a barge

Voici Paris vu de la tour Eiffel.

Les grandes rues s'appellent des
boulevards.

Au milieu de la photo il y a l'Arc de
Triomphe.

Napoléon a fait construire l'Arc de
Triomphe pour célébrer ses
victoires.

> vu – seen
> a fait construire – had built

As you listen to the tape, you should imagine that this French person is speaking directly to you and asking you a question. Your problem here is simple and urgent: you have a second or two in which to find some way of answering the question! Answer as fast as you can before the bleep! Don't worry about how accurate your French is; a French person listening to you wouldn't. Concentrate on getting your meaning across.

After a pause, you will hear an answer to the question, but it is only one **possible** answer, not the **only** answer possible. If you are not sure whether **your** answer makes sense, ask your teacher.

j'écris

Imagine that your school is setting up a link with a class in a French school. You have been asked to write a few brief details about yourself in French so that they can pair you off with a French pupil of your age.

Begin by giving your name, age and address and then write about your family, your likes and dislikes.

On se donne rendez-vous pour...

You will probably have come across the word *pour* in its usual meaning **for**. This is only **one** of its meanings. It often means **in order to** or just **to**.

*On va au cinéma **pour** voir un film.*

*On va à la piscine **pour** nager.*

*On va au théâtre **pour** regarder une pièce.*

*On va au restaurant **pour** manger un bifteck.*

*On va au café **pour** prendre une bière.*

*On va à la gare **pour** prendre un train.*

Try using *pour* by putting together some of these sentences:

Je vais	à la banque au café		prendre un café. rencontrer un ami.
Il va Elle va On va	à l'aéroport au port à la salle de concert à la piscine	pour	écouter de la musique. nager. chercher de l'argent. prendre l'avion.

In each case, *pour* is followed by the **doing word** (verb) in the form you will find in the dictionary. Here are some more which you might use:

manger	eat
regarder	watch
dormir	sleep
danser	dance
patiner	skate
nager	swim
marcher	walk
faire une promenade	go for a walk
boire	drink
voir un ami	see a friend
regarder la télé	watch TV

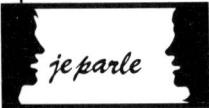

je parle   In French, say:

1 You're going to the bank to draw some money.

2 You're going to the hotel *(à l'hôtel)* to sleep.

3 You're going to the cinema to watch a film.

4 You're going to a town (you choose which) to buy something.

5 You're going somewhere (you decide where) for a walk.

6 You're going to the airport to catch a plane.

7 You're going somewhere (you decide where) to see a friend.

8 You're going to the station to catch a train.

9 You're going to a café, and say why.

10 You're going to leave *(je vais partir)* and say why.

You should now be able to:

1 say 'hello' when you meet someone for the first time;

2 ask and answer the usual questions when getting to know someone;

3 say what your mum or dad does for a living;

4 remember some other French words for jobs;

5 say what you like and don't like;

6 arrange a meeting;

7 ask and tell the time;

8 say why you want to go to some places;

9 remember the days of the week:

la
semaine

dimanche · lundi · mardi · mercredi · jeudi · vendredi · samedi

10 know the months of the year:

janvier
février
mars
avril
mai
juin
juillet
août
septembre
octobre
novembre
décembre

RÉPERTOIRE

Salutations

bonjour	hello
enchanté	pleased to meet you
ça va?	how are you?
salut	hello **or** goodbye
au revoir	goodbye

Véhicules

un vélo	a bicycle
un vélomoteur	a moped
une mobylette	a moped
un train	a train
un avion	a plane

Lieux

un collège	a school
une cour	a playground
une banque	a bank
un cinéma	a cinema
un stade	a sports ground
un hôtel	a hotel
une mairie	a town hall
une discothèque	a disco
une patinoire	a skating rink
une piscine	a swimming pool
un théâtre	a theatre
un restaurant	a restaurant
un café	a café
une gare	a station
un aéroport	an airport
un port	a port
une salle	a room

Où?

devant	in front of
derrière	behind
en face de	opposite
près de	near
à côté de	next to

Professions

un fermier	a farmer (man)
une fermière	a farmer (woman)
une secrétaire	a secretary
un routier	a lorry driver
une ménagère	a housewife
un maçon	a builder
un professeur	a teacher
un banquier	a bank employee
une infirmière	a nurse
une coiffeuse	a hairdresser (woman)
une informaticienne	computer technician

Actions

prendre	take
écouter	listen to
manger	eat
nager	swim
chercher	look for
regarder	watch
dormir	sleep
danser	dance
patiner	skate
marcher	walk
boire	drink
voir	see

Divers

j'aime	I like
je n'aime pas	I don't like
ces	these
après	after
une journée	a day
où	where

Finding a place to stay in a French town

You may well visit France as an *échangiste* (on a school exchange), or as part of a school visit. If you exchange with a French pupil you will live in her/his home as part of the family. On the other hand you may go on holiday and stay in a hotel, a tent or caravan or a youth hostel.

You may well go on holiday to France with your family and find yourself having to do the talking for all of you! We will look at how to find somewhere to stay using your French.

Cet hôtel s'appelle l'Hôtel l'Europe.
Il est en face de la gare.
C'est un bon hôtel.

Regardez bien la photo.
Est-ce que vous voyez la gare?

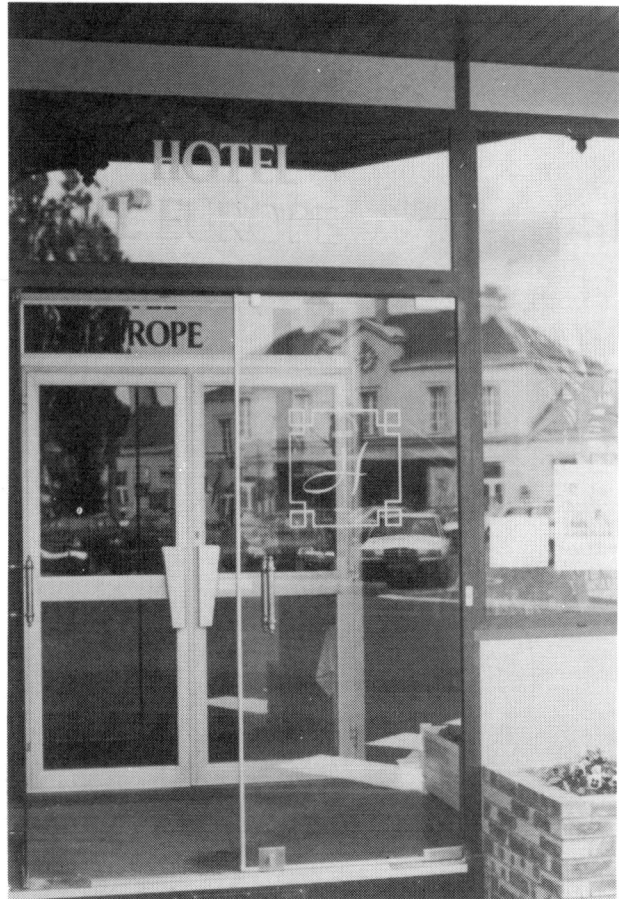

Je voudrais une chambre, s'il vous plaît.
I'd like a room, please.

Of course, you may need to change this a little. You may want **two** rooms (for other members of your family), or a room with a bath or shower. We will look at how to ask for the combination of rooms and beds that you need.

j'apprends

Here are some words which will be useful when it comes to finding your way round a French hotel.

RÉCEPTION

RC12345

le casier

la clef

l'ascenseur

SONNER S.V.P

le téléphone

l'escalier

la sonnerie

FICHE

Nom _____

Prénoms _____

Adresse _____

Date de naissance _____

Lieu de naissance _____

Nationalité _____

Numéro de passeport _____

Although they are no longer obliged to do this by law, some French hotels still ask their guests to fill in a *fiche,* a form like this one.

At some point during your visit to France you may have to fill in a form, so copy this *fiche* into your exercise book and then fill it in. It's pretty 'guessable' (and they're often printed in several languages, including English) but see how well you cope with the French alone! By the way, *lieu* means 'place'.

C'est l'intérieur d'un hôtel. C'est l'Hôtel l'Europe.
Voici le réceptionniste. C'est un jeune homme.
Derrière le réceptionniste il y a des clefs.
Sur le comptoir il y a des journaux.

Je voudrais une chambre...

Je voudrais	une chambre deux chambres	avec douche avec salle de bains avec bain avec un grand lit avec deux lits	pour une nuit deux nuits trois nuits	s'il vous plaît.

j'écoute A

You will now hear a series of ten people booking into a hotel.
Fill in your copy of the chart below to show exactly what they ask for.

	room (s)	beds	nights	other requests
1				
2				
3				
4				
5				
6				
7				
8				
9				
10				

Au camping...

You and your family may decide to go camping in France. It's worth knowing how charges are worked out. Check outside the campsite: there is a board which will tell you how these break down. Often, a separate charge is made for the vehicle you travel in, the number of people staying and *l'emplacement* (the site) the patch of ground on which you pitch your tent.

Voici un camping.
Il s'appelle le 'Camping de Ribou'.
Le camping est près d'un lac.

Au camping

Est-ce que vous avez de la place?		
Je voudrais un emplacement pour	*une tente* *deux tentes* *une caravane*	*s'il vous plaît.*
Nous sommes .... personnes et nous restons .... nuits.		

In the spaces you put the number of people and the number of nights.

je parle

With your partner taking the part of the receptionist, book yourself and your family into a hotel and a campsite following the instructions below:

1 Get a room for your family and yourself. Think about the kind of beds/rooms your family really need. Decide on whether you want a shower or a bathroom. Find out about breakfast and whether they serve an evening meal. Say you want to be woken up at 7.00 am. Say you're staying for four nights. Spell your surname to the receptionist. Ask where you can park your car:

Où est-ce qu'on peut garer la voiture?

2 Your family are touring with a caravan and a large tent. Book in to the campsite, then find out where the washing facilities and showers are. Ask if there is a shop on site.

Comment cela s'écrit?
How do you spell that?

You may well have a name that the French would not immediately recognise.
You may be asked *'Comment cela s'écrit?'* (How do you spell that?)

B j'écoute

Listen to the tape recording of the French alphabet and to your teacher.
Make a copy of this table in your exercise book and add your own guide to
the sounds. Answers for the first four have been suggested.

A	fAther		N	
B	**BA**y		O	
C	**SA**y		P	
D	**DA**y		Q	
E			R	
F			S	
G			T	
H			U	
I			V	
J			W	
K			X	
L			Y	
M			Z	

After the alphabet, the speaker will spell these words; *musique, cinéma, télévision,
radio, discothèque,* plus these British names: Brown, Smith, Lucas, Thomas and
Morris; then you will hear ten other words spelled out to you three times each. Try to
write these down in your exercise book!

DIRECTIONS >

Here are some signs that you might see whilst in a hotel or on a campsite.
You need to learn them.

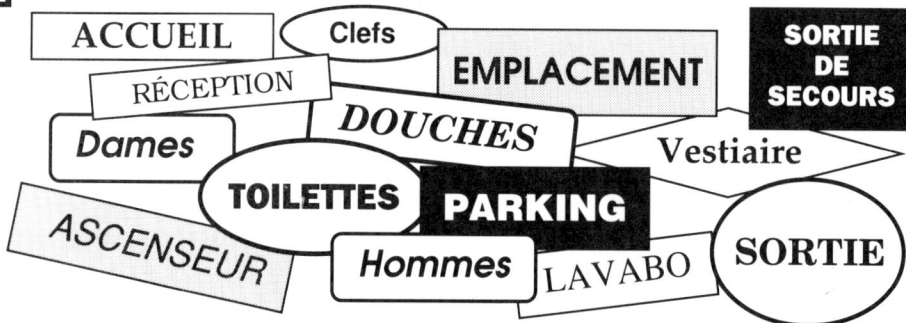

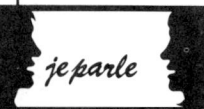

ACCUEIL   Clefs   EMPLACEMENT   SORTIE DE SECOURS

RÉCEPTION   DOUCHES   Vestiaire

Dames   TOILETTES   PARKING

ASCENSEUR   Hommes   LAVABO   SORTIE

je parle

Try asking for rooms with the six things shown below:

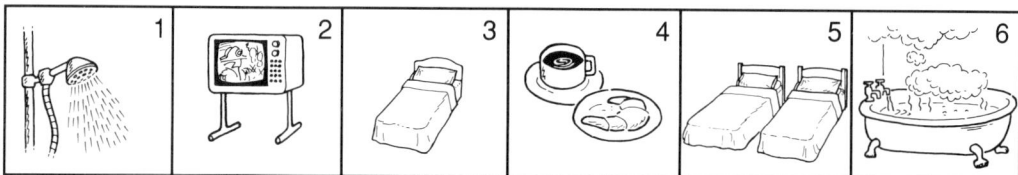

1	2	3	4	5	6

Je voudrais une chambre, s'il vous plaît.

Dialogue 1

Client	Bonjour, Madame.
Propriétaire	Bonjour, Monsieur.
Client	Je voudrais une chambre à deux lits pour mes parents et une chambre à un lit pour moi-même.
Propriétaire	Oui, Monsieur... pour combien de nuits?
Client	Pour deux nuits, s'il vous plaît.
Propriétaire	Très bien, Monsieur. Voici les clefs des chambres dix et onze. Si vous voulez bien remplir ces fiches...

Dialogue 2

Client	Bonjour, Madame... je voudrais une chambre à un lit avec douche, s'il vous plaît.
Propriétaire	Bien, Monsieur. Vous voulez le petit déjeuner, bien sûr?
Client	Oui, je veux bien; et un repas du soir, c'est possible?
Propriétaire	Oui, Monsieur, dans le restaurant de l'hôtel.

Dialogue 3

Cliente	Bonjour, Monsieur, je voudrais un emplacement pour une tente, s'il vous plaît.
Propriétaire	Oui, Madame. Vous avez une voiture?
Cliente	Oui.
Propriétaire	Et vous êtes combien?
Cliente	On est deux adultes et trois enfants.
Propriétaire	Et vous restez combien de nuits?
Cliente	On reste deux nuits.
Propriétaire	Alors... un emplacement, une voiture, cinq personnes pour deux nuits... cela vous fait cent quatre-vingts francs, Madame.

L'agriculture en France

L'agriculture est très importante en France.

Après la guerre, les champs étaient très petits.

Ce n'était pas bien. Les Français ont réuni beaucoup de petits champs.

Maintenant les champs sont plus grands et les fermes sont plus efficaces.

La France est le premier producteur de l'Europe de céréales.
La France est le premier producteur de blé, d'orge et de maïs.

PARIS

Le Bassin Parisien produit beaucoup de céréales.

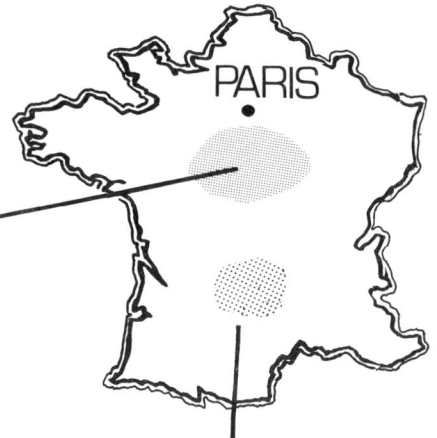

L'agriculture est difficile ici. Il y a beaucoup de montagnes. C'est le Massif Central.

après – after	réuni – brought together	l'orge – barley
la guerre – war	maintenant – now	le maïs – maize
le champ – field	plus – more	ici – here
était – was	efficace – efficient	la montagne – mountain
étaient – were	le blé – wheat	

France is very much an agricultural country, well able to support itself by growing its own food. The most important areas of the country for agriculture are the areas north of Paris, Brittany and the Parisian basin, which is called France's 'bread basket'.

It is important to realize just how large France really is. Take a look at a map of Europe and compare the size of France with the size of Great Britain.

je lis

Le vin

La bière est très importante en Angleterre, mais le vin est très important en France.

La France et l'Italie sont les deux producteurs de vin les plus importants du monde.

Sur cette petite carte on voit les régions les plus importantes pour la production du vin.

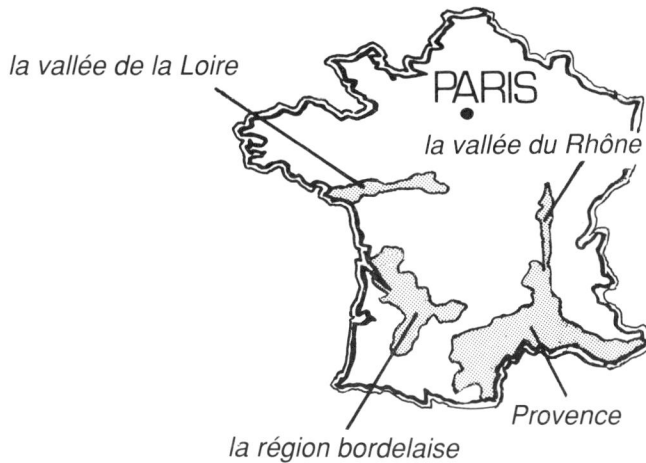

la vallée de la Loire

PARIS

la vallée du Rhône

Provence

la région bordelaise

Quel véhicule étrange! Qu'est-ce que c'est?
(Réponse à la page 31)

le/la	the
un/une	a

Let's look again now at something you will have come across right back in your first year of French. This is the idea that some words are **un** words and some are **une** words. In fact, all the words which describe things and objects fall into the one category or the other.

je révise
je révise
je révise

You may have been taught that these are **masculine** and **feminine** words.

The French person's universe

Unfortunately, there is no logical reason why a lake is **un** *lac*, while a river is **une** *rivière*.

That's just the way it is.

So how do you tackle this problem? Here are some tips:

1 However unreasonable it seems, try to learn the two together. Learn **un** *hôtel* and not just *hôtel*;

2 **People words** (**un** *père*, **une** *mère* and so on) are usually logical;

3 Don't panic! Even if you get it wrong you will still be understood!

You also need to know the difference between **un/une** and **le/la.** Look at the diagrams to the right.

une cassette
a cassette

la cassette
the cassette

je cherche

See how much you can decipher of this hotel bill. It could be yours and you'd need to check it. What extras are the customers being charged for?

HÔTEL - MOTEL ✶ ✶ NN
RESTAURANT - BAR
"LE PARASOL"
17590 ARS-EN-RÉ, Ile de Ré
Tél. (46) 29.46.17
R.C. 80 B 91 - APE 6708

FACTURE

M

le 23 Septembre 1986.

How to ask questions

When getting to know someone, it's important to show interest in **them**.

In other words, you need to be able to **ask** questions, as well as **answer** them.

Here are two techniques for putting questions to people. Suppose you want to know whether someone plays football or not. You can either say:

Tu joues au football?   You play football?

or else you can say:

Est-ce que tu joues au football?   **Is it that** you play football?

Both are used a lot by French people. Bear in mind, though, that you have to use a questioning **tone**, whichever technique you use. Your teacher will show you how this is done.

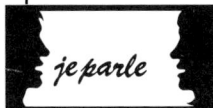

je parle   Use your French to find out whether your partner:

1 plays ...... (put in a sport)   6 speaks ...... (put in a language)
2 likes ...... (choose something)   7 plays ...... (put in an instrument)
3 eats ...... (put in a food)   8 likes ...... (put in a popstar)
4 lives in ...... (put in a town)   9 collects ...... (put in something)
5 likes ...... (put in a band)   10 drinks ...... (put in something)

Expressions utiles

tu manges	you eat	*tu habites à*	you live
tu collectionnes	you collect	*tu aimes*	you like
tu joues	you play	*tu parles*	you speak

j'apprends   Some questions need a **question word** to begin them.

où	where	*qui*	who
pourquoi	why	*comment*	how/what
quand	when	*quel (le)*	which

je travaille   Can you decide what these questions mean?

1 *Où est-ce que tu habites?*
2 *Pourquoi est-ce que tu portes un pullover?*
3 *Qui est dans la salle de bains?*
4 *Quand est-ce que tu vas au cinéma?*
5 *Quelle heure est-il?*
6 *Avec qui est-ce tu vas à la disco?*
7 *Qu'est-ce que tu portes ce soir?*
8 *Comment est-ce que tu t'appelles?*
9 *Qu'est-ce que tu manges?*
10 *Quand est-ce que 'Dallas' passe à la télé?*

je parle   Now put questions like these to your partner.

2

Expressions utiles

avec qui	with whom	*y a-t'il*	is there
as-tu	have you	*qu'est-ce que*	what is it that…
est-ce que tu veux	would you like to…	*est-ce que je peux*	may I
qu'est-ce tu veux	what would you like to…		

je travaille

Can you work out the details of these two bills?

Hôtel Bollenberg ★★

68250 ROUFFACH
Tél. (89) 49.62.47
BRC Colmar 916 720 832
Télex: 880 896 F BOLLENB

N° Chambre 26 - 27

M.
Le 2 - 09   19 84   165   330

Appartement:
2 ch.

Salon:

Bar: 60

Petit déjeuner: 3

Téléphone:

Divers:

RESTAURANT FERMÉ LE LUNDI TOUTE L'ANNÉE et LE DIMANCHE SOIR HORS SAISON
SAUF DU 1er JUILLET AU 1er SEPTEMBRE

MOTEL ★★ **L'EUROPÉEN RESTAURANT** S.A.

VOGELGRUN
Code Postal : NEUF-BRISACH 68600
à 200 m. des Écluses du Grand Canal
(HAUT - RHIN)
d'Alsace
RENÉ DAEGELE, P. D. G.
CHEF DE CUISINE

TÉLÉPHONE
(89) 72 51 57

Ses Vins
d'Alsace
et ses Spécialités
culinaires
Sa vue sur le Rhin
et Vieux - Brisach

R. C. COLMAR B 917020586
SIRET 917020580 00013
APE 6708

C. M. D. P. Bartholdi Colmar 3200.127506.45
B. P. N. B. 75 / 21 / 505.5623 .

FACTURE

N° 020726   pour   Le   9/08

2   ch. 10 - 11

3   274 —
                                      36 —
                                     29 0 0
                                     295 —
                                     583 0

SALLE DE SÉMINAIRE ET DE CONFÉRENCE

Work in pairs. One of you should look at **this** page and the other at page 160.

You are the receptionist at the Hôtel de Paris in Cholet. Below are the six rooms which are still vacant, together with the number of nights for which they are free. Your partner will play the parts of **six** customers: they will want different things. Your job is to accommodate them as best you can. Each moon sign represents one night.

Remember to be diplomatic! Your job is to stay calm and polite, however awkward things get. Your customers may not all be as pleasant as you would like! Your hotel needs the custom… it's been going through a bad patch recently!

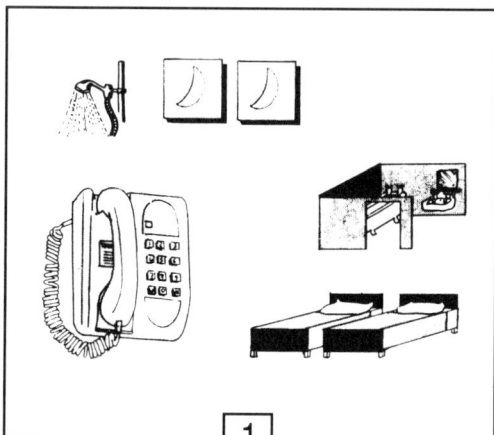

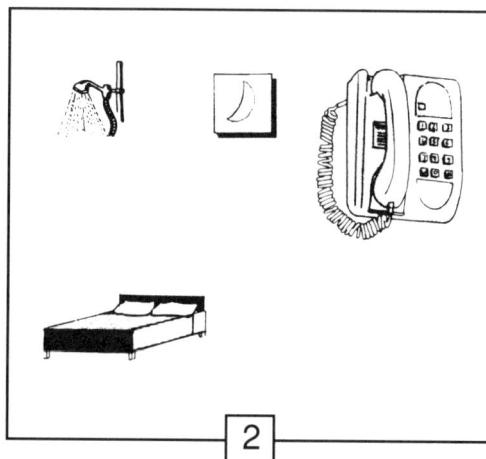

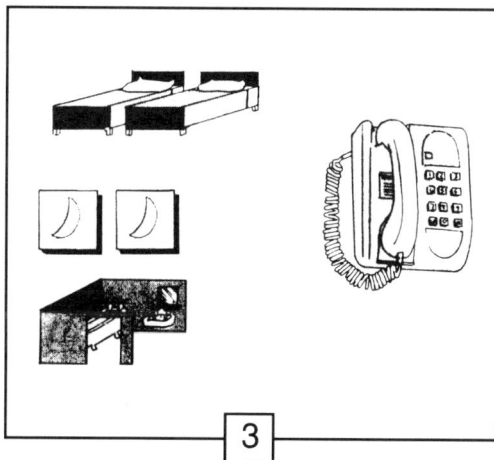

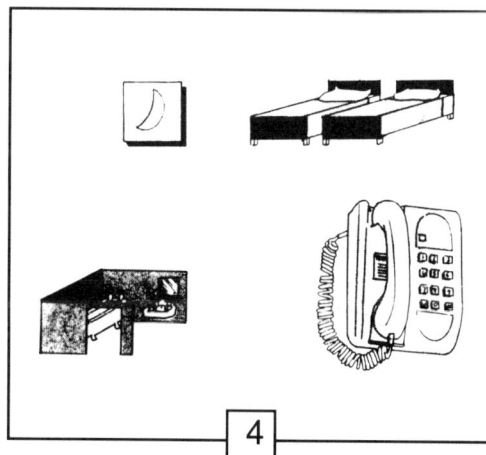

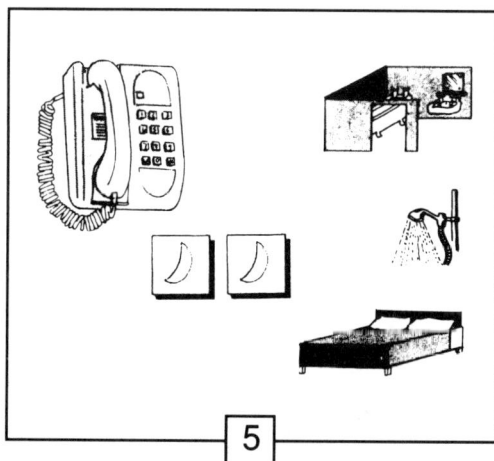

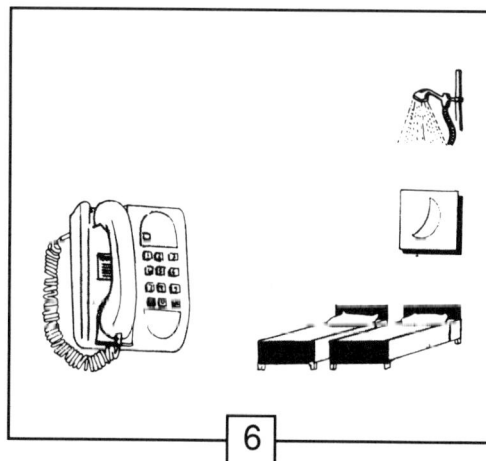

DIRECTIONS

SALLE DE SÉJOUR   SALON   OUVERT À CINQ HEURES   SORTIE

Salle de télévision   Fermé pour congé annuel   SALLE DE BAINS

BUREAU   RENSEIGNEMENTS   DAMES   FERMÉ POUR CONGÉ

SORTIE DE SECOURS   Il est interdit de marcher sur la pelouse   HOMMES

Expressions utiles

Est-ce que tu parles français?	Do you speak French?
Est-ce que tu parles anglais?	Do you speak English?
Tu comprends?	Do you understand?
Tu veux bien répéter ça s'il te plaît?	Would you repeat that, please?

Be ready for the *vous* versions of these:

Est-ce que vous parlez français?	Do you speak French?
Est-ce que vous parlez anglais?	Do you speak English?
Vous comprenez?	Do you understand?
Vous voulez bien répéter ça s'il vous plaît?	Would you repeat that, please?
Je ne comprends pas	I don't understand
Comment on dit 'sleeping bag' *en français?*	How do you say 'sleeping bag' in French?
Comment on dit 'sac de couchage' en anglais?	How do you say *'sac de couchage'* in English?
Qu'est-ce que ça veut dire?	What does that mean?
Que veut dire 'baguette'?	What does *'baguette'* mean?

trois... deux... un...TOP! D

Once again, you have a second or two in which to find some way of answering the questions you hear. This time you are booking in, first to a camp-site and then to a hotel. Answer as fast as you can before the bleep!

j'écris

1   Imagine that you are writing a letter to a French penfriend. Don't write the whole letter. Think about the sort of thing you might want to know about your correspondent and write a few questions which you might put into such a letter.

2   You want a summer job in France and so you write to an agency there. They send you a form. Fill in a copy of this.

Nom.............................Prénoms usuels......................................

Date et lieu de naissance...

Adresse..

Numéro de téléphone...

Personne à contacter en cas d'accident...

Numéro de la pièce d'identité..

You should now be able to:

1 say you would like a room at a hotel;

2 tell the receptionist what combination of rooms and beds you want and for how long;

3 book your family into a campsite;

4 spell your name in French, and recognise things spelled out aloud to you;

5 put questions to people, and know some of the more useful question words.

je travaille

French handwriting can be quite a problem!

Can you decipher these hotel bills?

RÉPERTOIRE

À l'hôtel

une chambre	a room
un casier	a pigeonhole
une clef	a key
une sonnerie	a bell
un téléphone	a telephone
un ascenseur	a lift
un escalier	a staircase
une douche	a shower
un bain	a bath
un lit	a bed
une sortie	an exit
des toilettes	toilets

Au camping

de la place	room/space
un emplacement	a site
dames	ladies
hommes	gentlemen
un lavabo	a washroom
un parking	a car park

Divers

un numéro	a number
jeune	young
un journal	a newspaper
une nuit	a night
un lac	a lake

RELAIS DU VIVARAIS

André ESPERANDIEU
PROPRIETAIRE
07220 Viviers-s-Rhône

BAR - HOTEL *A - RESTAURANT
R. C. Aubenas 60 A 621
C. C. P. LYON 1379-85
Téléphone (75) 49.60.41

Nationale 86

CHAMPAGNE "CREMANT BLANC"
BESSERAT de BELLEFON
Le vin de tout un repas...

Getting yourself something to eat and drink

You'll have to eat during your stay in France! If you are trying to get by on as little money as possible, your best bet is to buy food in a local supermarket; it's good, cheap, and makes a great picnic. However, you may like to try the famous French *cuisine* (many people would say that the French and the Chinese are the world's best cooks) so we will look at how to buy a meal.

je travaille

In the drawing below, you'll see a whole lot of things to eat and drink. Put the numbers (1 to 20) in your exercise book, then match up the letters of the French names which appear here:

a *du pain*
b *un poulet*
c *des escargots*
d *un petit pain au chocolat*
e *un yaourt*
f *un couvert*
g *du jambon*

h *un Orangina*
i *une tasse de café*
j *du melon*
k *un jus de fruit*
l *un verre de vin*
m *de l'eau*
n *le menu*

o *un plateau de fromages*
p *un potage (une soupe)*
q *des fruits*
r *du saucisson*
s *un sandwich*
t *de la choucroute*

If you're not going to buy food from a supermarket, it's generally cheapest to eat a snack in a café. If you decide to eat a meal in a café or restaurant, you have the choice of buying a set meal *(le menu à ... francs)* or choosing *à la carte*. This means you can choose anything that is on the menu, but it could be expensive.

When you want to call the waiter, don't click your fingers or shout *'garçon!'* Waiters don't always appreciate this (and you may have to take your soup externally!). It's best to say:

> *Monsieur, s'il vous plaît!*

or if a waitress is serving you:

> *Mademoiselle/Madame, s'il vous plaît!*

The meal itself will probably be in three or four parts. You will normally be expected to choose one item from each part of the menu. Slices of French bread (usually *baguette*, the stick loaf) will normally be placed on the table as well as *une carafe d'eau* (a jug of water). It's usual to put your bread on the tablecloth, rather than on a side plate.

The parts of a menu are usually as follows:

entrée	starter
plat principal	main dish *(le plat de résistance)*
fromages	cheeses, usually a wide variety
dessert	dessert

A *j'écoute* You'll now hear some people ordering various combinations of food. The menu they're choosing from is on page 32. Write down the number of each item as it is mentioned.

Here are the names of some desserts:

coupe glacée	various ice-creams in a dish
vacherin	meringue and ice-cream
poire belle hélène	pears with ice-cream and chocolate
profiteroles	choux pastry with ice-cream and melted chocolate
gateau forêt noire	Black Forest gâteau
plateau de fruits	various fruits

Le Relais du Vivarais

Answer to p 23 *Quel véhicule étrange!*
The vehicle is a vineyard tractor, shaped in such a way that it can pass easily between the rows of vines.

Soon you will be old enough to try the local beer. There are two main types: *la bière blonde* (light ale) and *la bière brune* (mild ale) and it is served either *en bouteille* (bottled) or *à la pression* (draught).

When ordering you can say:

Un demi, s'il vous plaît. (This gets you draught beer)

Une bière en bouteille, s'il vous plaît. (You've made it clear that you want bottled beer)

	ENTRÉES		
1	melon au porto		melon with port
2	oeufs mayonnaise		eggs with mayonnaise
3	assiette anglaise		various cold pork meats
4	escargots de Bourgogne		fresh Burgundy snails

	PLATS PRINCIPAUX		
5	poulet fermière		chicken
6	côte d'agneau provençale		lamb chop
7	truite aux amandes		trout served with almonds
8	omelette aux champignons		mushroom omelette

	FROMAGES		
9	le camembert		cheese from Normandy
10	le gruyère		cheese from Switzerland
11	le roquefort		made from ewe's milk
12	le brie		

	DESSERTS		
13	une salade de fruits		
14	un flan au caramel		caramel custard
15	une tarte de saison		a tart made with whatever fruit is available at the time
16	une glace		

Comme
by way of/in the way of

*Qu'est-ce que vous voulez **comme** dessert?* for example means 'What would you like by way of a dessert?' But you might find this expression useful in places other than restaurants and cafés.

*Qu'est-ce que vous voulez **comme** pain?*	What kind of bread do you want?
*Qu'est-ce que vous voulez **comme** chemise?*	What sort of shirt do you want?

It may be used when someone asks you about the kind of thing you want to buy. But you will find it useful yourself when you want to find out what is available:

*Qu'est-ce vous avez **comme** fromages?*	What sort of cheese do you have?
*Qu'est-ce vous avez **comme** boissons?*	What kinds of drink do you have?

Qu'est-ce que vous	*avez* *voulez*	*comme*	*hors d'oeuvres?* *desserts?* *boissons?* *fromages?* *bière?* *gâteaux?* *vins?*

je parle

You and your partner should now take it in turns to play the parts of waiter/waitress and customer. As the waiter/waitress, you will have to think up the replies.

1 Find out what kinds of cheese they have in this restaurant.
2 Find out what sandwiches they do in this café.
3 Find out what snacks they serve in this café.
4 Find out what hot drinks *(boissons chaudes)* they serve here.
5 Find out what white wine they serve here and then order a bottle.
6 Find out what desserts this restaurant is offering and then order one.

Now use this block diagram to help you order things.

Je prendrai (I'll have…)	*le menu à*	*trente* *quarante* *cinquante* *soixante*	*francs, s'il vous plaît.*

How to say you're hungry or thirsty

J'ai	*faim.* *soif.*

I'm hungry.
I'm thirsty.

Listen carefully to the way your teacher pronounces these. You can use the same technique when you want to say that someone else is hungry or thirsty:

Il a *Elle a*	*faim.* *soif.*

He/she is hungry.
He/she is thirsty.

je parle

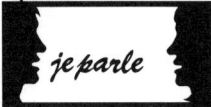

Call the waiter/waitress over! One of you is the waiter/waitress. Both of you should be very polite (don't forget *Monsieur/Mademoiselle*). Order a full meal *à la carte.* Use the menu to help you. Order drinks too. When ordering the various parts of the meal, don't forget to use **comme** to find out what's on offer!

Expressions utiles

Ce sera tout?	Will that be all?
Et comme boisson?	And by way of a drink?
Vous avez choisi?	Have you made up your minds?

When you have finished your meal...

...you will have to deal with what is sometimes called *la douloureuse*, (the painful one). This is a way of saying 'the bill'. Its real name is *l'addition*.

You need to be able to say:

> *Monsieur, s'il vous plaît? L'addition, s'il vous plaît.*

*je révise
je révise
je révise*

Here is a reminder about how to talk about what people are going to do. The question would be:

Qu'est-ce que tu vas	*faire?* *prendre?*

The answer could be:

Je vais *Il va* *Elle va*	*manger au restaurant.* *boire un café.* *aller au café.* *chercher son frère.* *acheter une robe.* *prendre un Orangina.*

Je vais means 'I am going', so if you say ***Je vais manger***, this will mean **I'm going to eat**.

Here are some more examples. See if you can understand them!

1 *Je vais acheter un journal; puis je vais manger au café.*
2 *Il va aller au musée avec sa soeur.*
3 *Elle va aller à Monoprix pour acheter une jupe.*
4 *Je vais boire une bière à la pression.*
5 *Je vais regarder la télévision ce soir.*

One of you asks the questions below.

The other person has to answer the questions using the expressions you were shown on the previous page. If you need to, you should have another look at that page now… but don't use it when you're answering the questions.

1 *Qu'est-ce que tu vas prendre?*
2 *Qu'est-ce que tu vas manger?*
3 *Qu'est-ce que tu vas boire?*
4 *Qu'est-ce que tu vas acheter?*
5 *Où est-ce que tu vas aller?*
6 *Qu'est-ce qu'il va manger ?*
7 *Qu'est-ce qu'elle va boire?*
8 *Où est-ce qu'elle va aller?*
9 *Qu'est-ce qu'il va acheter?*
10 *Qu'est-ce que tu vas prendre?*

} replace *il/elle* with a name

L'eau minérale (mineral water) is sold everywhere in France. In some parts of France it is a good idea to buy mineral water because the local tap water may be suspect. Watch out for signs reading *'eau non potable'* which means it is not drinking water. Common brands of mineral water sold in all French supermarkets include:

VICHY VITTEL PERRIER
THONON EVIAN BADOIT.

In France, large numbers of people go off to stay at spa towns such as Vichy and Royat, in the centre of the country, to get themselves cured of all manner of illnesses by drinking special mineral waters.

As a patient in a spa town you are given a little leather box, which is circular in shape and can sometimes even be locked with a little padlock. Inside is a measuring jar to show how many centilitres of each of the spa waters you are to take in order to cure your liver problem, for example.

The healing power of mineral water is said to come from the different minerals contained in the various types of water. Not everyone believes this.

Qu'est-ce qu'on prend?

Dialogue 1

Marie	Monsieur, s'il vous plaît?
Garçon	Oui, Mademoiselle? Qu'est-ce que je vous sers?
Marie	Je prendrai le menu à 40 francs, s'il vous plaît.
Garçon	Le menu à 40 francs, bien Mademoiselle. Vous voulez quelque chose à boire?
Marie	Un jus de pamplemousse, s'il vous plaît.
Garçon	Un jus de pamplemousse. Bien, Mademoiselle.

Dialogue 2

Jean	Madame, s'il vous plaît?
Serveuse	Oui, Monsieur?
Jean	Je voudrais une assiette anglaise…
Serveuse	Oui, Monsieur, et avec ça?
Jean	Après, je prendrai un bifteck.
Serveuse	Bien, Monsieur. Et comment vous le voulez, votre bifteck?
Jean	Saignant.
Serveuse	Vous voulez un dessert?
Jean	Qu'est-ce que vous avez comme desserts?
Serveuse	Glaces, crème au caramel, plateau de fruits…
Jean	Je prendrai une crème au caramel… et puis un café.

Dialogue 3

Garçon	Madame?
Mme Noiray	Alors, Jean, qu'est-ce qu'on prend?
M. Noray	Je prendrai une bière…
Garçon	À la pression ou en bouteille, Monsieur?
M. Noiray	À la pression, s'il vous plaît.
Garçon	Et pour vous, Madame?
Mme Noiray	Je prendrai un café crème.
Garçon	Bien… une pression, un crème.

je lis

La France touristique

Les spécialités régionales

tarte
aux poireaux

coquille dieppoise

jambon
des Ardennes

quiche lorraine

soupe de poisson
à la normande

crêpes bretonnes

coupe champenoise

choucroute
alsacienne

rillettes du Mans

poisson au
beurre blanc nantais

fondue
bourguignonne

sauce berrichonne

gratin
dauphinois

entrecôte
bordelaise

potée auvergnate

omble-
chevalier du lac

tourte cantalienne

gigot à la provençale

truffes
du Périgord

cassoulet toulousain

bouillabaisse   ratatouille niçoise

poulet à
la basquaise

tarte catalane

Chaque région de la France a ses spécialités gastronomiques. Si tu vas en Bretagne, par exemple, tu vas aimer les crêpes. 'Crêpe' se dit 'pancake' en anglais. Si tu vas en Alsace, tu vas peut-être manger de la choucroute. 'Choucroute' se dit 'sauerkraut' en anglais (et en allemand!).

Find out:

1 what *truffes* are, where and how they are found;
2 how a *fondue bourguignonne* is eaten;
3 how a *ratatouille* is cooked;
4 what is in a *coquille dieppoise* (or *coquille St Jacques*).

France is famous for its wine and cheese. There are hundreds of each of these but only a very few appear on this map. Cider is not a wine, of course. It's included here because Brittany is France's Somerset, as far as cider is concerned.

Le vin et le fromage

Pont l'évêque

Sylvaner

Camembert

Brie

Champagne

Munster

Cidre

fromages de chèvre

Bourgogne

Muscadet   Touraine

Clairette

Bleu d'Auvergne

St. Nectaire

Tomme

Roquefort

Côtes du Rhône

Reblochon

Bordeaux

Châteauneuf du pape

fromages de chèvre

Cahors   Rosé de Provence

fromages des Pyrénées

La nourriture est très importante en France: le vin et le fromage sont encore plus importants! Il y a des vins blancs, des vins rouges et des vins rosés. Certains vins sont pétillants, comme le champagne ou la clairette. Il y a des fromages forts, comme le roquefort, et des fromages doux, comme le fromage de chèvre.

la nourriture – food
encore plus – even more
pétillant – sparkling
fort – strong
la chèvre – goat

DIRECTIONS

ATTENDEZ ICI

SERVICE À L'APPRÉCIATION
DE LA CLIENTÈLE

SERVICE 15%
COMPRIS

SORTIE
INTERDITE

LES CHIENS
NE SONT PAS
ADMIS

Issue de secours

Restaurant au
premier étage

TÉLÉPHONES

Plats chauds à emporter

Qu'est-ce que tu vas faire plus tard?

Look back at page 34, where you learned how to say what you're going to do. You can
use this technique for saying what you want to do when you leave school. You might
be asked:

> Qu'est-ce que tu vas faire après le collège?
> Qu'est-ce que tu feras quand tu quitteras le collège?

Both of these mean:

> What are you going to do when you leave school?

Here are some possible answers, some of which use *devenir*, which means 'to
become':

Je vais devenir maçon.	I'm going to become a builder.
Je vais devenir secrétaire.	I'm going to become a secretary.
Je vais travailler dans un magasin.	I'm going to work in a shop.
Je vais continuer mes études.	I'm going to continue my studies.

Your teacher will tell you any words you need in order to say what you're going to do
when you leave school.

*trois... C
deux...
un...TOP!*

Once again, you have a second or two in which to find some way of
answering the question! You'll find it useful to look at the menu on page 32
as you do this. This time you are in a restaurant. Answer as fast as you can,
before the bleep!

j'écris

You are writing to a French friend: write just that part of the letter in which
you tell your friend about some of the things which you plan to do during
the coming weekend. Don't write the whole letter.

Work in pairs. One of you should look at **this** page and the other at page 161.

You are a customer in a restaurant in Paris. Your partner will play the part of the waitress or waiter. The menu appears below. You have 100 francs to spend on your meal. Begin by choosing what you want to eat and then:

1 call the waitress or waiter over politely;

2 order your meal, being ready to change your mind if need be;

3 ask what drinks are available (don't forget **comme**);

4 when the main course has been served, complain that it is too cold!

5 ask for the bill, and offer to pay using travellers' cheques (*les chèques de voyage*).

When you finish, turn to page 161 and play the other part.

MENU

	ENTRÉES		
1	melon au porto		15F
2	oeufs mayonnaise		15F
3	assiette anglaise		20F
4	escargots de Bourgogne		35F

	PLATS PRINCIPAUX		
5	poulet fermière		35F
6	côte d'agneau provençale		40F
7	truite aux amandes		45F
8	omelette aux champignons		25F

	FROMAGES		
9	le camembert		10F
10	le gruyère		10F
11	le roquefort		15F
12	le brie		10F

	DESSERTS		
13	une salade de fruits		15F
14	un flan au caramel		10F
15	une tarte de saison		10F
16	une glace		10F

Expressions utiles

…est trop froid	…is too cold
je voudrais payer par chèque de voyage	I would like to pay by traveller's cheque

You should be able to:

1 read a simple menu;

2 order a set meal or *à la carte;*

3 ask what kinds of cheese, wine and so on are served in a restaurant;

4 say that you are hungry or thirsty;

5 say what you're going to do;

6 say what someone else is going to do.

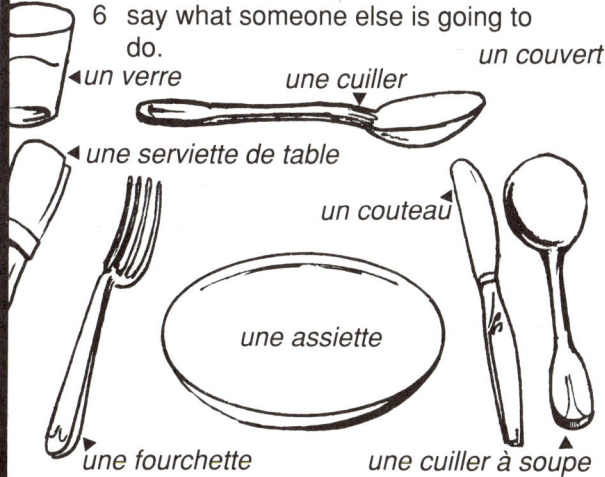

un verre ◄

une cuiller

un couvert

une serviette de table ◄

un couteau

une assiette

une fourchette

une cuiller à soupe

RÉPERTOIRE

Nourriture

du pain	bread
du poulet	chicken
des escargots	snails
un yaourt	yoghourt
un couvert	a place setting
du jambon	ham
une tasse	cup
un café	coffee
du melon	melon
un jus	a juice
un verre	glass
de l'eau	water
un plateau de fromages	cheese plate
un plateau de fruits	fruit bowl
un potage	soup
de la choucroute	sauerkraut
la carte	menu
une entrée	starter
un plat	dish
un oeuf	egg
une assiette	plate
de l'agneau	lamb
une truite	trout

Boissons

une bière	beer
une bière blonde	a light ale
une bière brune	mild ale
à la pression	draught
en bouteille	bottled

Divers

un cadenas	a padlock
une sacoche	leather bag
le cuir	leather
avez	you have
prenez	you take

RESTAURANT *Rech* 1925

Huîtres · Coquillages
Crustacés · Poissons
et son Camembert

62, avenue des Ternes,
75017 PARIS
Tél. 45 72 29 47 & 45 72 28 91

Fermé le Dimanche

R.C. Seine 60 B 5145

		NO	14
		TABL	•0.00
		NO	14
		TABL	•0.00
H.O.	•68.00		
H.O.	•66.00		
VIANDE	•180.00		
BOISS/	•99.00		
DESSER	•40.00		
DESSER	•25.00		
CAFE	•24.00		
		TOTL	•502.00
			73.00
05-08-87			

BOISS/	•55.00		
BOISS/	•38.00		
		TOTL	•93.00
05-08-87			

RESTAURANT RECH
5 AOUT 1987

Auberge du Parvis

Edwige et Francis SCHMIDT
Propriétaires

1, place Saint-François 74000 Annecy
Salle climatisée

tél.
50 45 03 05
Fermé le mercredi

l'Alsace

BRASSERIE-RESTAURANT

39, CHAMPS-ÉLYSÉES
PARIS 75008
TÉL. 43.59.44.24

Ouvert jour et nuit
dégustez et emportez
nos choucroutes
et spécialités régionales

Here are advertisements for two restaurants and a bill from another. How much can you understand of them?

How to buy things in different kinds of shop

We are going to look at a few techniques that will make shopping in France easier. In supermarkets and hypermarkets in France, as in England, you can get away with the occasional grunt at the cash-desk! Many shops still give a personal service, however, and you'll find that your French gets you what you want more quickly, and it often helps you get **exactly** what you want where there's a choice.

First of all, do you remember one of the most useful expressions you've come across?

> *Je voudrais*   I would like...

You can use it in all kinds of situations. Don't forget to add *'s'il vous plaît'* and use *Monsieur, Madame* and *Mademoiselle* properly when speaking to the shopkeeper. It is also usual to say *'au revoir'* when you leave the shop.

Supermarkets and hypermarkets in France can be huge. You can save yourself a lot of time if you can ask for the department *(le rayon)* you want:

> *Où se trouve le rayon ...... s'il vous plaît?*
> Where is the ...... department please?

The name of the department you're looking for goes into the gap, of course.

je travaille   Can you match up the French names for departments with the English ones?

le rayon		department	
1	*boucherie*	a	butter and cheese
2	*charcuterie*	b	grocery
3	*beurre et fromage*	c	household goods
4	*boulangerie*	d	dairy foods
5	*épicerie*	e	butcher
6	*fruits et légumes*	f	bakery
7	*produits ménagers*	g	fruit and vegetable
8	*produits laitiers*	h	pork butcher
9	*papeterie*	i	drinks
10	*boissons*	j	stationery

Au supermarché

je travaille

Without looking back to the last page, can you say to which *rayons* (departments) the six **lettered** sets of shelves in this picture belong?

What would you expect to buy in the three *rayons* at the back of the store?

The trolley is called *un chariot* or *un caddie*.

je lis

Voici le rayon des vins dans un grand supermarché en France.
Le vin est une des richesses de la France.
Il y a de nombreuses variétés de vin.

une des richesses – one of the riches
nombreuses – many

est	sont
is	are

If you want to say that someone **is** tired, tall, blond, stupid, pretty or that some things **are** large, expensive, red or new, then you need the French words **est** and **sont**.

You also need some **describing words** (adjectives). Have a look at these sentences and see if you can understand what is being said here:

1 *La voiture **est** rapide.*
2 *Les robes **sont** chères.*
3 *Le café **est** chaud.*
4 *Le train **est** en retard.*
5 *Les disques **sont** mauvais.*
6 *Les garçons **sont** au cinéma*
7 *Le sandwich **est** grand.*
8 *La bière **est** bonne.*
9 *L'hôtel **est** confortable.*
10 *Les filles **sont** intelligentes.*

cher – dear	*en retard* – late
chaud – hot	*bonne* – good

je parle

With your partner, see if you can describe anything or anyone you can see now, using the **describing words** (adjectives) above. If you need more, you can find others on page 80.

je lis

Voici des sacs à main sur un étalage de marché.
La plupart des sacs sont noirs et blancs et se portent en bandoulière.

Les prix varient entre 50F et 100F.

un étalage – a stall
la plupart – most
se portent – are worn
en bandoulière – on a shoulder strap

French supermarkets and hypermarkets have some rather odd names! Here is a selection: RALLYE MAMMOUTH EUROMARCHÉ SUPER-U
RADAR SHOPI CARREFOUR

je lis

Voici le rayon des vêtements dans le supermarché Rallye à Cholet.
Les vêtements sont souvent moins chers dans les supermarchés.
La dame à gauche a mis son petit garçon dans son chariot.

Voici le rayon charcuterie.
Au rayon charcuterie, il y a de la viande de porc et des plats préparés.

Alsacienne in this photo means 'from Alsace', a region near the border with Germany where they are particularly good at preparing pork dishes.

4

It's often useful to be able to make quite clear to the shopkeeper **which** item you want when there is more than one to choose from. The box below shows you which word to use.

celui-ci	*celle-ci*	= this one
celui-là	*celle-là*	= that one
LE words	**LA** words	

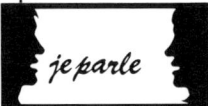

je parle

1 With your partner, take it in turns to play the part of a shopkeeper and a customer. Buy one of each of the items shown below, but make sure it's really the one you want!
2 Repeat the practice exercise above, but this time imagine a different shop (perhaps a clothes shop) and practise choosing particular items using *celui-ci, celui-là, celle-ci* and *celle-là*.

la bouteille	le beurre	le paquet	le stylo	la poire	la brosse	la cassette	la montre

Here is a reminder about how to buy a **quantity** of something:

Je voudrais	une livre un kilo une boîte un paquet un bocal une bouteille	de	....	s'il vous plaît.

Je voudrais un kilo de beurre, s'il vous plaît.
Je voudrais une livre de fromage, s'il vous plaît.
Je voudrais une bouteille de vinaigre, s'il vous plaît.

un tournevis
un marteau
une scie
une vis
un canif

je révise
je révise
je révise

1 You enter a small grocer. Your partner is the shopkeeper. Buy all the things you need for a picnic.

2 A table has collapsed in your caravan. Your partner is the shopkeeper in a *quincaillerie* (hardware shop). This picture will help you decide what you need to ask for.

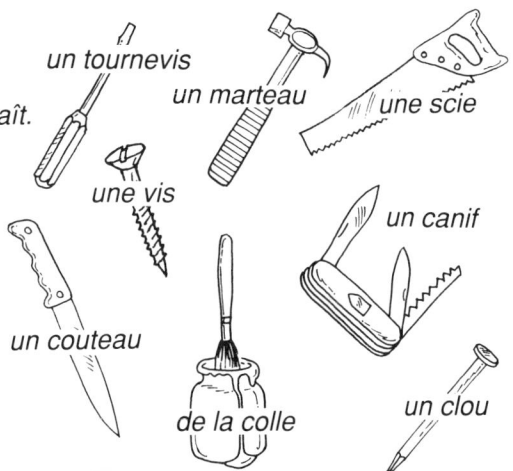

un couteau
de la colle
un clou

How to say what you are doing, or what someone else is doing

je mange	I'm eating	I eat
il mange	he's eating	he eats
elle mange	she's eating	she eats
on mange	we're eating	we eat

Listen carefully to the way your teacher says these words.

tu manges	you are eating	you eat
vous mangez	you are eating	you eat

Look at page 49 to see when to use *tu* and *vous*.

Here are some other **doing words** (verbs) which you can use in the same way:

je regarde	I'm watching	I watch
je travaille	I'm working	I work
je parle	I'm speaking	I speak
je roule	I'm driving	I drive
je nage	I'm swimming	I swim
je joue	I'm playing	I play
je cherche	I'm looking for	
j'aime		I like

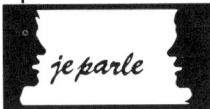

je parle

Work with your partner. Use the expression *Qu'est-ce tu...*
(What do you ...) to find out:

1 What your partner watches on TV.
2 What your partner eats in the evening.
3 What sport your partner plays.
4 What subject your partner likes.
5 What singer your partner likes.

je lis

Dans un supermarché, beaucoup d'enfants jouent avec les ordinateurs le samedi.
La même chose se passe dans les librairies: les enfants lisent des bandes dessinées tout l'après-midi!

jouent – play
un ordinateur – computer
la même chose – the same thing
se passe – happens
une bande dessinée – cartoon

Can you eat it or drink it?!

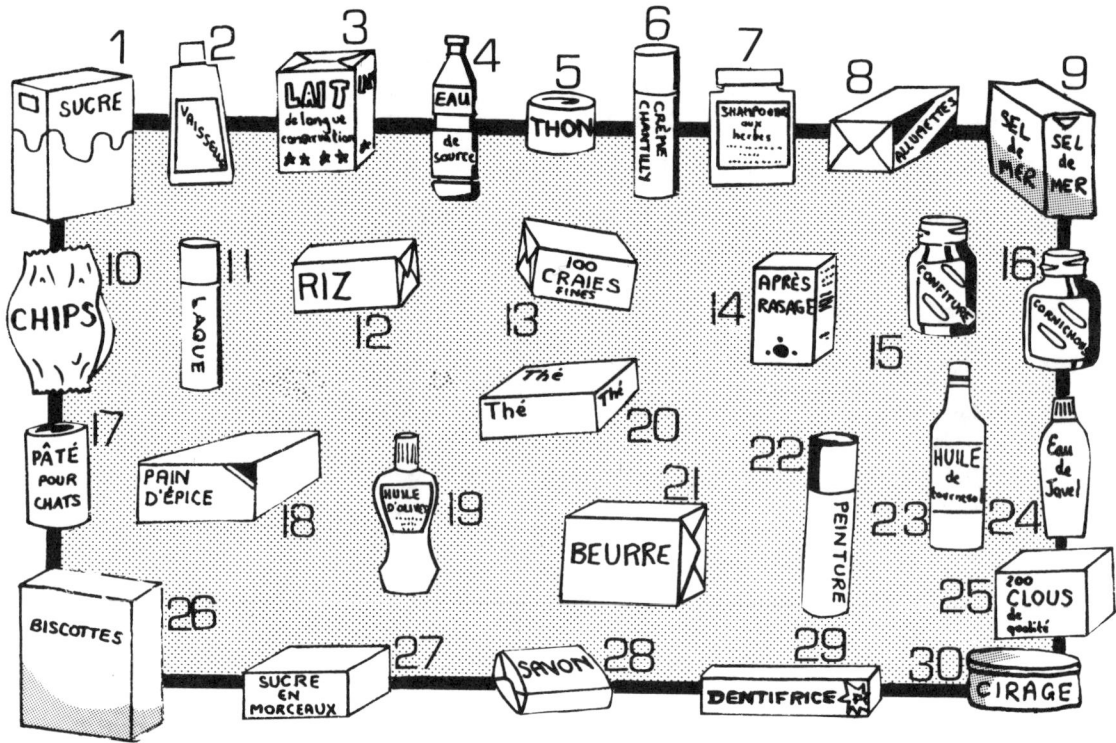

When you go to buy things in a supermarket it is not always obvious what a packet contains. For example, there is a bottle labelled *Fruit d'or* with what looks like an orange slice on it so you might think it's orange juice, but you'd be wrong. In fact the bottle contains cooking oil! So you can see how important it is that you can read the labels on packets.

Imagine that you've just entered a French supermarket: you're very hungry and thirsty. You must buy five things to eat and one to drink from the items illustrated here. Copy the chart below into your exercise book and fill in the numbers of the items you choose. You **must** eat and drink what you buy! When the whole class has finished deciding what to buy, your teacher will be able to tell you who's still alive… and who's got bad stomach-ache!

drink	food				
1	1	2	3	4	5

Les magasins et les boutiques

je travaille

Can you match up the French names for shops with the English ones?

1	*le magasin de sports*	a	bookshop
2	*la boulangerie*	b	household products
3	*la quincaillerie*	c	pork butcher
4	*la papeterie*	d	supermarket
5	*la charcuterie*	e	hardware store
6	*l'épicerie*	f	paper shop
7	*la librairie*	g	grocer
8	*la droguerie*	h	sports shop
9	*le supermarché*	i	stationery shop
10	*le magasin de journaux*	j	bakery

You may have noticed that the French have three types of butcher:

la charcuterie	a butcher specialising in pork
la boucherie	a general butcher
la boucherie chevaline	a horse-meat butcher. (More about this elsewhere in this book.)

j'écoute **A**

You're going to hear ten people asking their way to various *rayons* in a supermarket. Copy the chart below in to your exercise book and put the number of the conversation to show that you understand which department has been asked for by each customer:

boissons	*fruits et légumes*
charcuterie	*produits ménagers*
épicerie	*beurre et fromage*
boulangerie	*papeterie*
produits laitiers	*droguerie*

For each of the conversations, jot down notes in English in your exercise book to show that you have understood:

1 what kind of shop is involved;   2 what was bought there.

How to say 'you'

tu is used when talking to **one** person you know well, to people of your own age or to members of your family.

vous is used when talking to one person you **don't** know well, for people older than you, or for whom you should show respect.

vous is used when talking to more than one person.

je travaille

Try to decide whether you would speak to the following using *tu* or *vous*. You'll have to guess at some of them.

1 your French friend
2 the president of France
3 your French friend's stick insect
4 the head teacher of the French school
5 the bouncer at the local night-club
6 a boy at the French school whom you detest

Combien je vous dois?

Dialogue 1

Client	Vous avez des bananes, s'il vous plaît?
Vendeuse	Oui, Monsieur. Combien en voulez-vous?
Client	Je prendrai une livre de bananes et puis un kilo de raisin.
Vendeuse	Oui...ce sera tout?
Client	Vous avez du beurre?
Vendeuse	Bien sûr...combien en voulez-vous?
Client	Une plaque.

une livre – a pound (about 500g)
un kilo – a kilo
je prendrai – I'll have
une plaque – packet/slab

Dialogue 2

Client	Où sont les produits ménagers, s'il vous plaît?
Serveuse	Là-bas, à gauche, Monsieur. Près du rayon papeterie.
Client	Et les yaourts?
Serveuse	Ils sont au rayon des produits laitiers, Monsieur, sur la droite.
Client	Merci bien, Mademoiselle.

Dialogue 3

Client	Qu'est-ce que vous avez comme gâteaux, s'il vous plaît, madame?
Serveuse	J'ai des mille-feuilles, des religieuses, des petits fours, des babas au rhum...
Client	Je prendrai deux mille-feuilles, s'il vous plaît.
Serveuse	Bien, Monsieur. Ce sera tout?
Client	Oui. Combien je vous dois?
Serveuse	Alors, cela vous fait 12 francs, Monsieur.
Client	Voilà.
Serveuse	Merci, au revoir, Monsieur.
Client	Au revoir, Madame.

Work in pairs. One of you should look at **this** page and the other at page 162.

There are four people in your French correspondent's family and you have been asked to do the shopping at the local grocer. You have been asked to buy:

1 coffee
2 cheese (200 g)
3 a melon
4 a bottle of milk
5 ice-cream (you choose the flavour – but first find out what is available)
6 a magazine

Your partner will tell you the cost of each item. You have just 90 francs, so don't overspend! Make sure that everything you buy is in good condition.

Here is what's on offer.

When you finish, turn to page 162 and play the other part.

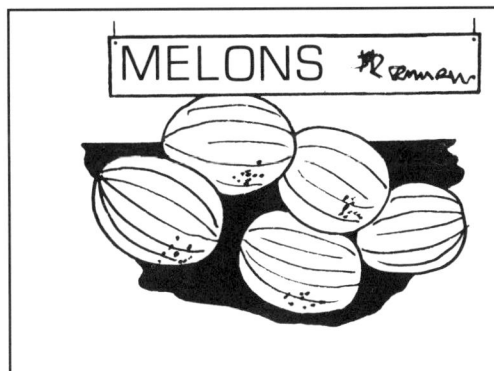

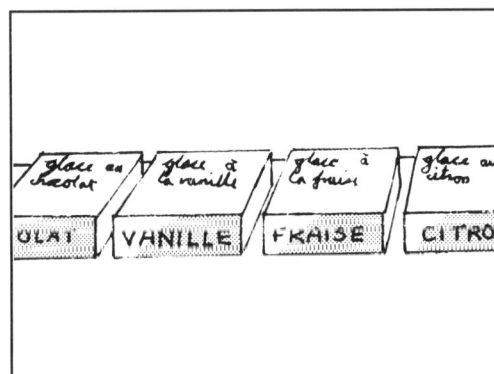

*trois... C
deux...
un...TOP!*

Once again, you have a second or two in which to find some way of answering the question! You are doing some shopping. Answer as fast as you can before the bleep!

j'écris

You are writing to a French friend: write just that part of the letter in which you tell your friend about the sort of thing you do in the evening. Don't write the whole letter.

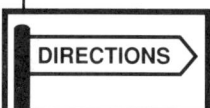

DIRECTIONS ⟩

INFORMATION

PRENEZ UN CHARIOT

Caisse

SOLDES

Les chèques ne sont pas acceptés pour tout règlement inférieur à cent francs

PRIX CHOC

Cafétéria au cinquième étage

SURVEILLANCE PAR TÉLÉVISION

ESCALIER ROULANT

Voici une boucherie chevaline. On y vend de la viande de cheval.

La boucherie ouvre à 7h15 et ferme à 12h45. Elle ouvre de nouveau à 14h45 (le déjeuner est important!) et ferme définitivement à 19h00.

La boutique est fermée les jeudi et samedi après-midi.

ouvert

LE MATIN
de ... à ...

L'APRES-MIDI
de ... à ...

fermé le

JEUDI | APRES-MIDI
SAMEDI | APRES-MIDI

La boucherie vend aussi de la charcuterie (la viande de porc) de la dinde et du chevreau. La dinde se dit 'turkey' en anglais et le chevreau se dit 'kid'.

PRIX DE VENTE
LE KILO

le filet – tender loin
le tournedos – fillet steak
le bifteck – steak
la viande – meat
la langue – tongue
le foie – liver
le coeur – heart
la cervelle – brains
les rognons – kidneys
les poumons – lungs

You should now be able to:

1 recognise a wide variety of shops from their French names;

2 recognise a wide variety of supermarket departments;

3 buy things in a shop;

4 ask your way to a particular supermarket department;

5 say which of a pair of things you want to buy using **celui-ci/là, celle-ci/là**;

6 say you want a certain quantity of a product.

RÉPERTOIRE

Magasins et rayons

une boucherie	butcher
une charcuterie	pork butcher
une boulangerie	bakery
une épicerie	grocer
une papeterie	stationery shop
un supermarché	supermarket
une quincaillerie	hardware store
un magasin	shop
une librairie	bookshop
une droguerie	household products

Nourriture

le beurre	butter
le fromage	cheese
le fruit	fruit
le légume	vegetable
la boisson	drink
la viande	meat
le porc	pork
la poire	pear

Divers

un chariot	trolley
cher	dear, expensive
celui-ci/celle-ci	this one
celui-là/celle-là	that one

Quantités

une livre	a pound (500g)
un kilo	a kilo
une boîte	box/tin
un paquet	packet
un bocal	jar
une bouteille	bottle

je lis

Voici une rue commerçante de la ville Vichy.

Il y a beaucoup de gens parce que c'est la période des vacances. En plus, c'est la période du tour de France.

Le monsieur de la camionnette vend des vélos miniatures aux passants.

commerçant – shopping
gens – people
un passant – a passer-by

How to find your way round a French town

We are going to look at how you find your way around a town and how to find the tourist office.

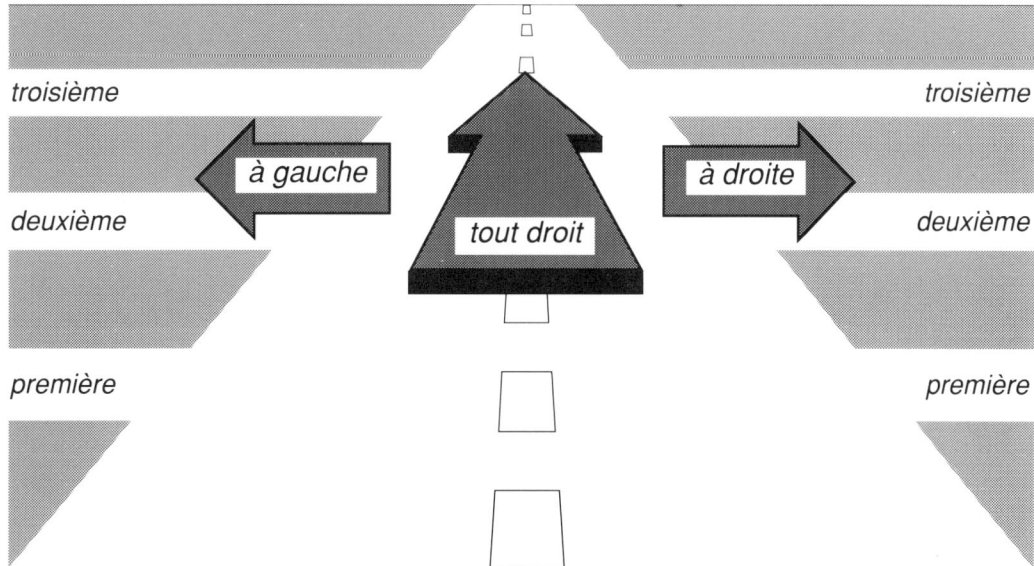

troisième   troisième

à gauche   *à droite*

deuxième   *tout droit*   deuxième

première   première

j'apprends

The phrases in the diagram above are vital for understanding directions (or for giving them to a French tourist whom you may meet in **your** town). Make sure you are familiar with them.

Giving directions to places

You may be given these instructions, or need to give them yourself:

prenez	take
allez	go
tournez	turn
continuez	continue
montez	go up
descendez	go down (go along)
traversez	cross
sur la gauche	on the left
sur la droite	on the right
pas loin de	not far from
tout près de	close by

> ## *Excusez-moi, Madame, pour aller à …… s'il vous plaît?*
> Excuse me, how do I get to …… please?

Into the blank goes the place you want to get to, of course!

Don't forget to be especially polite when stopping someone in the street to ask them the way; they may not be sure what you want! The first thing to say is *'pardon'*, *'excusez-moi'* or *'s'il vous plaît'*. Then add *'Monsieur, Madame'* or *'Mademoiselle'*.

> ## *On va en ville…*

j'apprends

Make sure you're very familiar with the following vocabulary.

le words

S.I.	*le syndicat d'initiative* (tourist office)
	le garage
	le port
	le café
	le restaurant
P	*le parking*
	le collège
	le supermarché
	le cinéma
	le théâtre
	le musée
POLICE	*le commissariat de police*
	le stade
	le bureau des objets trouvés

la words

	la banque
SNCF	*la gare*
	la mairie (town hall)
	la poste
	la pharmacie
	la pâtisserie
	la boucherie
	la piscine
	la boulangerie
	la patinoire
	la confiserie
	la droguerie
	la boucherie chevaline
	la gare routière

À la boulangerie

You've probably heard of the famous French stick loaf *(la baguette)* but perhaps you didn't know how many different kinds of bread there are in a typical bakery. Most bread in France is not made in a factory, but in the shop where you buy it. It's made fresh every morning. So it's worth getting up early to go and get some bread, hot from the oven!

The best thing to try is a *baguette*, or, if you prefer brown bread, a *pain complet*.

You'll notice that the bakery in our pictures calls itself a *pâtisserie* and a *confiserie* as well. Do you know what it is likely to sell, apart from bread?

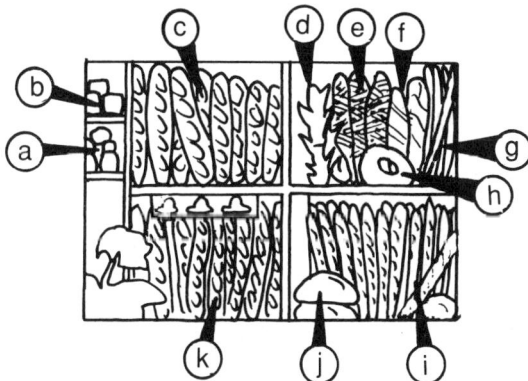

a   *pains de mie*
b   *pains de seigle*
c   *une flûte*
d   *un épi*
e   *pains parisiens*
f   *un pain*
g   *baguettes moulées*
h   *une couronne*
i   *baguettes*
j   *boules*
k   *flûtes*

The word *baguette*, the French name for the typical French stick loaf, means a 'wand'. The smaller version of it is called *la ficelle* which means 'string'.

In the picture below you'll see some *petits pains au chocolat* (on the far left of the picture). These are sweet rolls with sticks of chocolate running through the middle. To the right of them are some *croissants* which are part of the continental breakfast consisting of a hot drink, (coffee, hot chocolate or tea) jam and bread or croissants. Can you understand the notice on the right in the photo? It's an advertisement for *pains rustiques* (country loaves).

Au petit déjeuner en France on mange souvent des croissants ou des petits pains au chocolat.
Certains Français aiment les 'Cornflakes' mais beaucoup préfèrent le petit déjeuner traditionnel.

> *on mange* – people eat

Voici une rue à Cholet, une ville en France.
Un monsieur va traverser la rue.
En face du monsieur il y a un panneau électronique qui donne des informations sur la ville de Cholet.

A
j'écoute

You will hear a series of ten conversations. People have asked the way to one of the places on the map below. Your job is to decide **where** they wanted to get to! Copy the chart below into your exercise book and fill it in to show that you understand where they wanted to go. They all start from **X**.

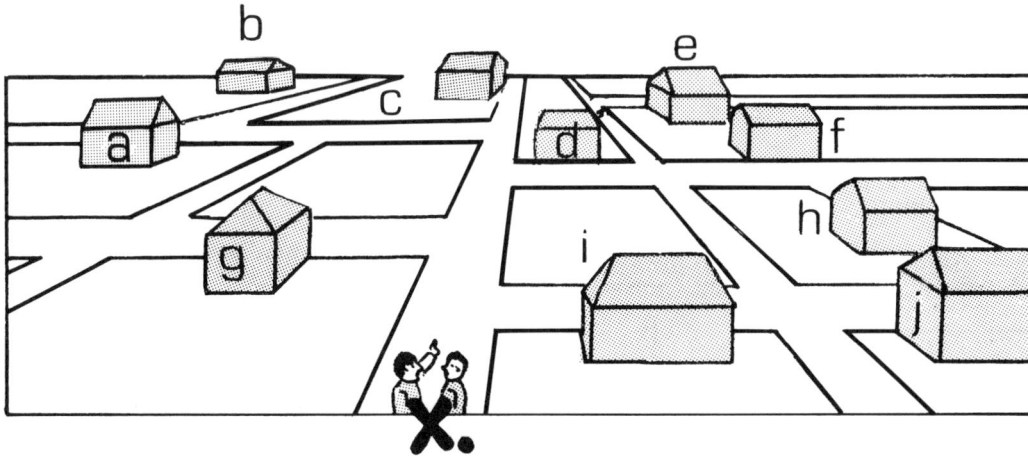

1	2	3	4	5	6	7	8	9	10

Expressions utiles

As has already been mentioned, it's particularly important to be polite when approaching a stranger in the street. Here are some more expressions which you can use when they seem appropriate:

s'il vous plaît	please
excusez-moi	excuse me
merci beaucoup	thank you very much
c'est très gentil	that's very kind of you
de rien	not at all (don't mention it)
je vous en prie	not at all (don't mention it)
vous ne pouvez pas vous tromper	you can't miss it
vous y êtes	you're there
c'est bien la direction de…?	is this the right way for…?
c'est loin d'ici?	is that far (from here)?

Link words

Have you noticed the two different ways of saying **to the** in these sentences?

> Pour aller **à la** poste, s'il vous plaît?
> Pour aller **au** camping, s'il vous plaît?

à la is used with **la** words *(la piscine)*
au is used with **le** words *(le stade)*

If you manage to get this right, well done! If not, don't worry, you will still be understood.

je parle

With your partner, take it in turns to begin from each of the black dots (start points) and direct each other to the numbered places as follows:

```
 1  a – 3
 2  b – 8
 3  c – 2
 4  d – 2
 5  e – 1
 6  f – 4
 7  a – 5
 8  b – 1
 9  c – 6
10  d – 7
```

Now go back to the previous page and, with your partner, practise directing each other to some of the places on the map.

Make an effort to get your conversation to sound as **real** as possible.

Use as many of the *Expressions utiles* on page 59 as you can (where these seem to fit).

Now go back to the lists of places to which you might direct people (on page 56) and practise directing each other to some of them, while trying to choose the right **link words** for **to the.**

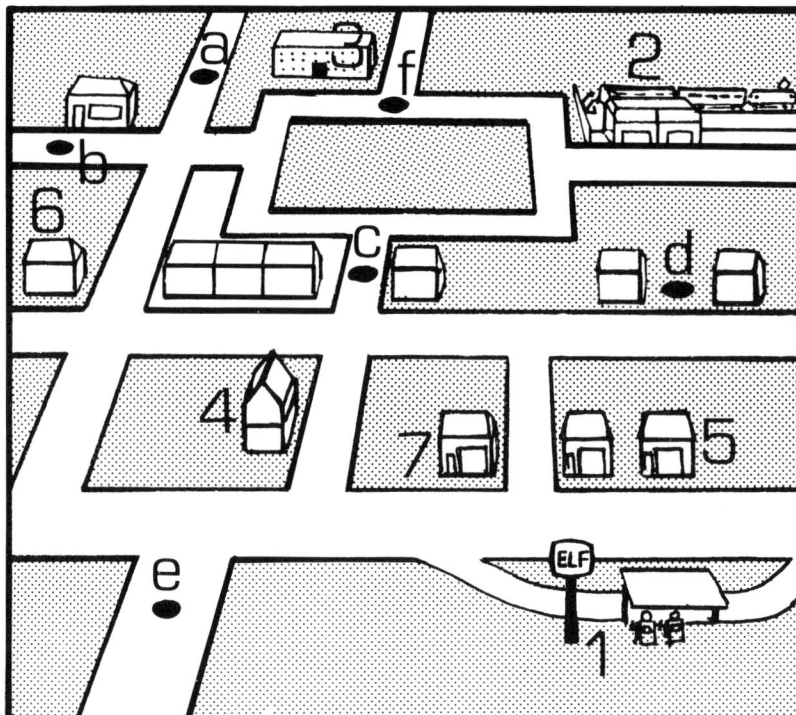

Talking about people and objects

When you're talking about **more than one** of anything, you need to know the French words for **some** and **the**:

des cassettes
some cassettes

les cassettes
the cassettes

As in English you usually add an 's' when there is more than one thing or person.

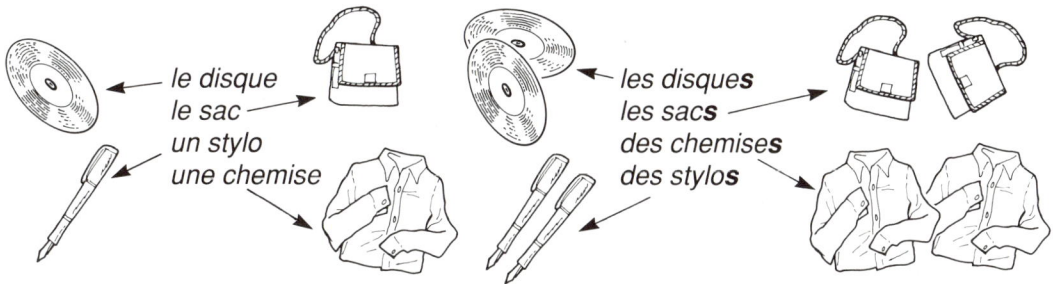

le disque
le sac
un stylo
une chemise

les disques
les sacs
des chemises
des stylos

Watch out! Just as in English you don't say sheeps, mouses or mans, in French there are many words which don't just add an 's' where there is more than one thing or person.

Here are a few examples:

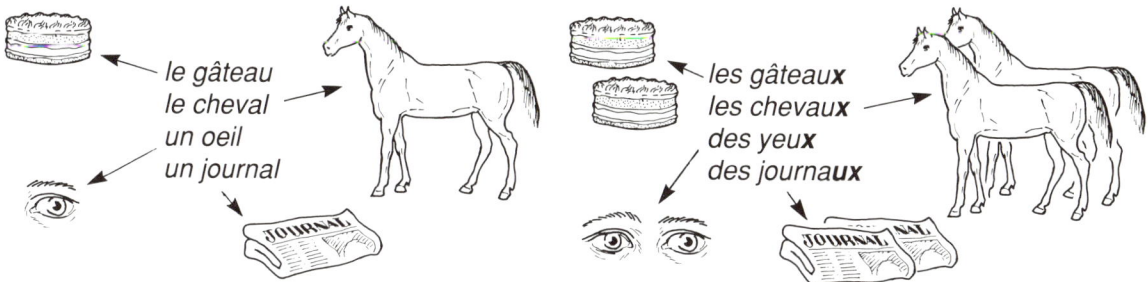

le gâteau
le cheval
un oeil
un journal

les gâteaux
les chevaux
des yeux
des journaux

je parle

Imagine that someone needs to buy the things shown below. You and your partner can pretend to be shopkeeper and customer. Using *des* (which means 'some'), ask for these things. But remember you need more than one of each.

un bonbon

une fraise

une chaussette

un biscuit

une chaussure

une allumette

Work in pairs. One of you should look at **this** page and the other at page 163.

In this game, you are visiting a French town. Ask your partner how to get to the places shown below and write down the numbers that correspond to them:

the station   the grocer   the bakery   the pork butcher   the police station

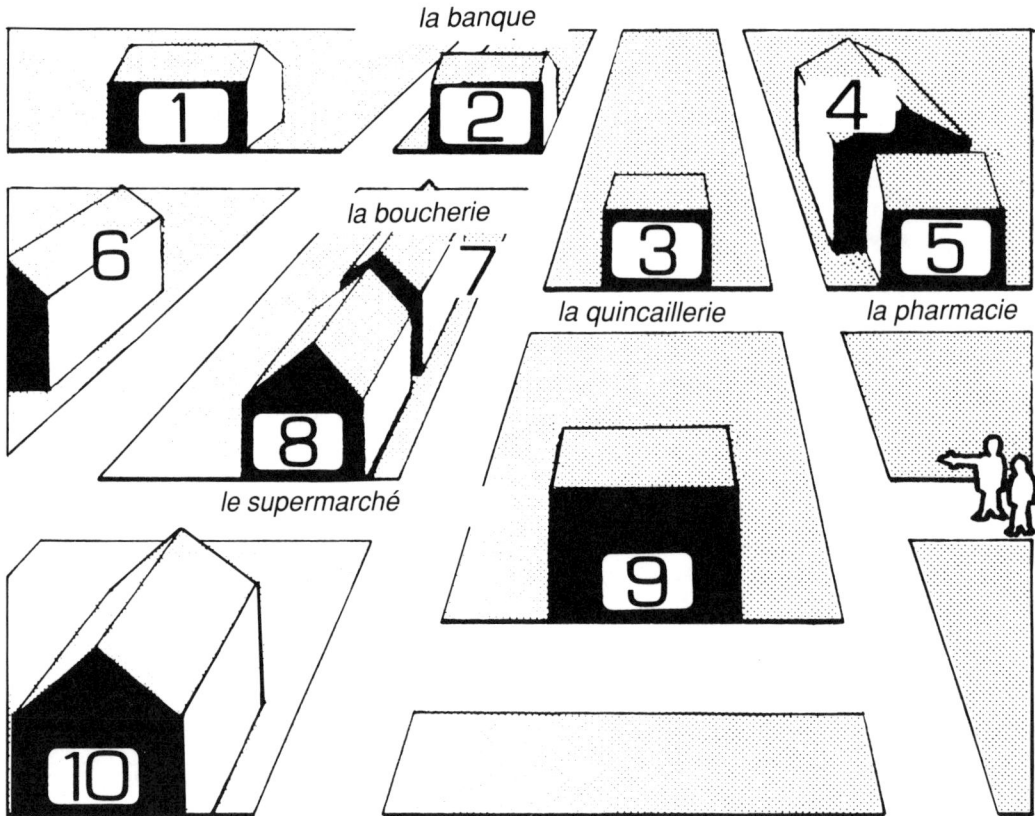

la banque

la boucherie

la quincaillerie

la pharmacie

le supermarché

Next your partner will ask you the way to the five places that are already marked on your map. Give her or him directions as if you were standing where the two people are.

How to say what you are not doing, or what someone else is not doing

> *ne ...... pas*

This expression means **not**. To use it, you put it round the **doing word** (verb) you're using, rather like a sandwich:

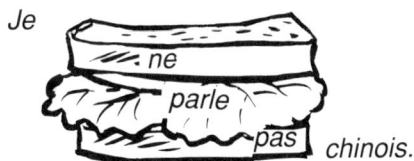

Je

ne
parle
pas *chinois.*

I don't speak Chinese.

If the **doing word** (verb) you are using begins with the letters a, e, i, o, u or h you need to use

> *n' ...... pas*

Je

n'
aime
pas *les escargots.*

I don't like snails.

je travaille

Can you decide what these mean?

1 *Je ne regarde pas 'Dynasty'.*
2 *Il ne parle pas anglais.*
3 *Elle ne joue pas au ping-pong.*
4 *Il ne nage pas dans la mer.*
5 *Je ne mange pas de salami.*
6 *Elle n'aime pas le chocolat.*
7 *Il ne mange pas de pommes de terre.*
8 *Il n'aime pas les carottes.*
9 *Je ne parle pas à Jeanne.*
10 *Elle ne joue pas au hockey.*

je parle

In French, say:

1 Your brother doesn't like ... (a record)
2 You don't talk to ... (a person)
3 You don't like eating... (think of something)
4 You don't play... (a sport)
5 You don't speak... (a language)
6 You don't like... (a school subject)
7 You don't watch... (a TV programme)
8 Your friend doesn't eat... (think of something)
9 She/he doesn't like... (a TV programme)
10 She/he doesn't play... (a sport)

Here are some more **doing words** (verbs) which you need to learn.
They don't work quite like the ones we've seen so far.

I'm going	*je vais*
I'm drinking	*je bois*
I'm taking	*je prends*
I'm writing	*j'écris*
I'm reading	*je lis*
I'm putting (putting on)	*je mets*
I'm coming	*je viens*
I understand	*je comprends*
I know (a person)	*je connais*
I have to (do something)	*je dois*
I know (something)	*je sais*
I see	*je vois*
I want	*je veux*

je travaille

Can you see what these sentences mean?

1 *Je vais à Oxford mardi.*
2 *J'écris une lettre à Pierre.*
3 *Je lis un livre.*
4 *Je connais Madonna.*
5 *Je veux un gâteau.*
6 *Je mets un pullover.*
7 *Je ne sais pas.*
8 *Je comprends le message.*
9 *Je prends une pilule.*
10 *Je viens samedi à une heure.*

j'apprends

Some **doing words** (verbs) are a bit awkward but **very** useful!
Learn these bits and pieces carefully:

je vais	I go	I am going
il va	he goes	he is going
elle va	she goes	she is going
on va	we go	we are going
tu vas	you go	you are going
vous allez	you go	you are going

je travaille

See if you understand what these mean:

1 *Il va au collège.*
2 *Marie va à Basingstoke.*
3 *On va au cinéma?*
4 *Elle va à la piscine.*
5 *Il ne va pas à la disco.*
6 *On va à la patinoire.*
7 *Elle va à la boucherie.*
8 *Je ne vais pas au supermarché.*
9 *Il va à la boucherie chevaline.*
10 *On va à l'épicerie.*

Au syndicat d'initiative

A quick way of finding out about important or interesting things to see and do in a French town that you're visiting for the first time is to go to the *syndicat d'initiative.* You'll find one of these in most French towns. Sometimes they're called the *Office du Tourisme.* Here are some of the things you may expect to find there:

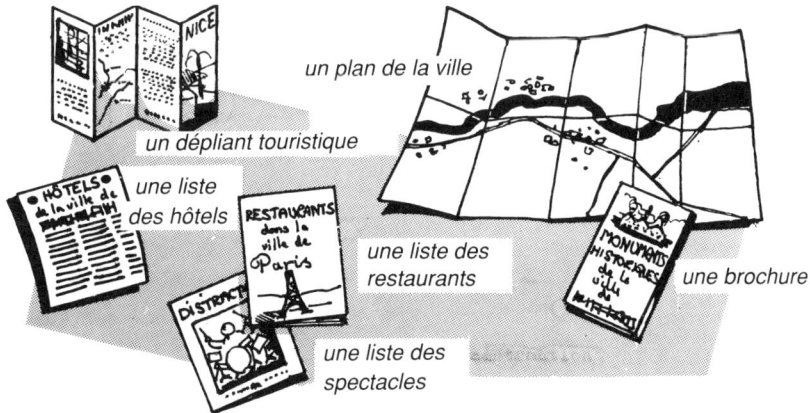

un plan de la ville

un dépliant touristique

une liste des hôtels

une liste des restaurants

une brochure

une liste des spectacles

Most French towns have a tourist office. It is usually found near the station or in the centre of town. There you can get information about where to stay and what to look at whilst staying in the town. Information leaflets are usually free of charge, although you can buy detailed books too. The tourist office will often find a hotel for you and make a telephone booking.

You can also write to the tourist office before leaving Britain and they will send you information to help you plan your stay.

This is the international sign for a tourist office. It stands for 'Information'.

Voici le syndicat d'initiative de la ville de Cholet. C'est une ville assez importante.

important means 'big' here.

Avez-vous...

In order to be able to ask for the various things offered in a *syndicat d'initiative* you need to say:

Avez-vous	une brochure touristique une liste des hôtels un plan de la ville une liste des restaurants une liste des campings	s'il vous plaît?

Other useful questions are:

Qu'est-ce qu'on peut faire le soir à ......? What can you do in the evenings in ......?
Où est-ce qu'on peut manger pour pas trop cher? Where can you eat fairly cheaply?
Qu'est-ce qu'il y a à voir dans la ville? What is there to look at in the town?
C'est gratuit? Is it free of charge?

B
j'écoute   You'll now hear ten people asking for various things in a tourist office. On your copy of the chart below, write what each customer wants.

customer	request
1	
2	
3	
4	

Ces deux dames travaillent dans le syndicat d'initiative de la ville de Cholet.

DIRECTIONS

SYNDICAT D'INITIATIVE:
20 MÈTRES SUR LA GAUCHE

CENTRE VILLE

EMPRUNTEZ LE PASSAGE SOUTERRAIN

OFFICE DU TOURISME

VOIE SANS ISSUE

MUSÉE À 500 MÈTRES

Servez-vous

Mairie

Où est-ce que tu passes tes vacances?
Where do you spend your holidays?

…au bord de la mer?

…à la montagne?

…au bord d'un lac?

…à la campagne?

j'apprends

Here are some useful expressions for talking about your holidays:

Je vais à Blackpool.	I go to Blackpool.
Je suis allé à Blackpool.	I went to Blackpool.
Je vais aller à Blackpool.	I'm going to Blackpool.
Je passe deux semaines à Blackpool.	I'm spending two weeks in Blackpool.
J'ai passé deux semaines à Blackpool.	I spent two weeks in Blackpool.
Je vais passer deux semaines à Blackpool.	I'm going to spend two weeks in Blackpool.

je parle

You and your partner should take it in turns putting any of these questions below to each other, and answering them by finding an answer from those above that seems right and changing it to suit your holiday plans. Change the times of year to suit yourself.

1 *Où est-ce que tu passes les grandes vacances?*
Where are you spending the summer holidays?

2 *Où est-ce que tu as passé les vacances de Noël?*
Where did you spend the Christmas holidays?

3 *Où est-ce que tu vas passer tes vacances cette année?*
Where are you going to spend your holidays this year?

4 *Où est-ce que tu as passé les vacances de Pâques?*
Where did you spend the Easter holidays?

5 *Où est-ce que tu vas passer les grandes vacances?*
Where are you going to spend the summer holidays?

6 *Où est-ce que tu passes les vacances de février?*
Where are you spending the holiday this February (half term)?

trois... deux... un...TOP!

Once again, you have a second or two in which to find some way of answering the questions that various people ask you. A party of French tourists has just got off their bus in your home town, or a town near where you live, and they have some questions for you. Do what you can to help them out! Answer as quickly as you can before the bleep!

j'écris

As part of a letter which you are writing to a French friend, tell your friend about the town or village where you live. You may like to mention the sort of thing you do there at the weekend, too. Don't write the whole letter.

je lis

A British tourist wrote to a tourist office to book accommodation in Les Portes en Ré. Can you understand the reply he received?

Syndicat d'Initiative
≡ BUREAU DU TOURISME ≡
de
LES PORTES EN RÉ   17880

Tél. (46) 29.52.71

Le...

Monsieur,

J'ai le regret de vous informer que je n'ai aucune location correspondant à votre demande.

Avec nos regrets, je vous prie d'agréer, Monsieur   , l'expression de mes sentiments distingués.

La secrétaire,

C'est loin d'ici?

Dialogue 1

Monsieur	Pardon, Mademoiselle, je cherche la gare.
Jeune femme	La gare? Eh bien, vous prenez la première rue à gauche, vous continuez jusqu'aux feux, puis vous tournez à droite et vous prenez la deuxième rue à gauche.
Monsieur	Alors, la première à gauche, je continue jusqu'aux feux, puis je tourne à droite et je prends la deuxième à gauche.
Jeune femme	Voilà.
Monsieur	Merci beaucoup, Mademoiselle.
Jeune femme	De rien, Monsieur.

Dialogue 2

Dame	Pardon, Monsieur, pour aller au cinéma Rex, s'il vous plaît.
Gendarme	Le cinéma Rex? Eh bien, vous prenez la deuxième rue à gauche, puis la deuxième à droite, et c'est en face de la pharmacie.

Dialogue 3

Jeune homme	Pardon, Madame, pour aller au Club 747, s'il vous plaît.
Dame	Voyons, le Club 747…vous continuez tout droit jusqu'aux feux…vous êtes à pied?
Jeune homme	Oui.
Dame	Hmm…c'est assez loin…après les feux vous tournez à droite…vous continuez jusqu'au garage Renault, puis vous tournez à gauche et le Club est à 100 mètres sur votre droite.
Jeune homme	Merci beaucoup, Madame…alors, je continue jusqu'aux feux, puis je tourne à droite, puis à gauche au garage et c'est à 100 mètres sur ma droite.

You should be able to:

1 stop someone in the street without alarming them!
2 ask your way to a place in town;
3 give and understand instructions concerned with directions;
4 ask for useful items in a tourist office;
5 make it clear whether you want one thing or more than one thing;
6 say what you or someone else is **not** doing;
7 say where you or someone else is **going.**

je cherche

Here are some extracts from a *dépliant touristique* (a tourist brochure). Find enough things to visit and enjoy to keep you going for a five-day visit.

votre santé est à Vichy!

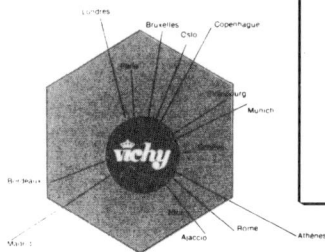

RÉPERTOIRE

Lieux publics

la station service	garage
le port	port
le café	café
le parking	car park
le collège	school
le cinéma	cinema
le théâtre	theatre
le musée	museum
le commissariat	police station
le stade	stadium
la banque	bank
la gare	station
la mairie	town hall
la poste	post office
la pharmacie	chemist's
la pâtisserie	cake shop
la boucherie	butcher's
la piscine	pool
la boulangerie	baker's
la patinoire	skating rink
la confiserie	sweetshop
la droguerie	household product shop
la gare routière	bus station

Directions

à gauche	left
à droite	right
tout droit	straight on
prenez	take
allez	go
tournez	turn
continuez	continue
montez	go up
descendez	go down
traversez	cross
sur la gauche	on the left
sur la droite	on the right
pas loin de	not far from
tout près de	close by

Au syndicat d'initiative

un plan	a map
un dépliant	a brochure

sports — détente

- PISCINES :
  - Municipale :
    Stade Nautique de Bellerive - Tél. (70) 32.27.20 & (70) 32.27.46
    - 1 bassin Olympique climatisé
    - 1 bassin couvert climatisé
  - Sporting Club : Pont de Bellerive - Tél. (70) 32.25.20
    - 1 bassin climatisé (Club-House)
- TENNIS :
  - Sporting Club : Pont de Bellerive - Tél. (70) 32.25.20
    - 12 courts terre battue
    - 4 courts porosol
    - 2 courts couverts terre battue } Abonnements
    - Stages
    - Professeur
- SQUASH :
  - Squash Club de Vichy - Tél. (70) 31.05.80
  - « Le Sunset » : Creuzier-le-Neuf - Tél. (70) 98.66.95
  - Centre Omnisports Pierre COULON - Tél. 32.04.68
    - 18 courts (3 nocturnes) - location à l'heure
    - Stages
    - Professeur
- GOLF :
  - Sporting Club : Pont de Bellerive - Tél. (70) 32.25.20
    18 trous - par 70 - Professeur
    Club-House avec restaurant - Tél. (70) 32.03.53
- SKI NAUTIQUE — VOILE — PLANCHE A VOILE :
  - Base Municipale de Voile :
    (Passeport Sportif du Centre Omnisports) - Tél. (70) 32.04.68
  - Yacht-Club de Vichy :
    Boulevard de Lattre-de-Tassigny - Tél. (70) 98.73.55
- PASSEPORT SPORTIF :
  Pour les moins de 18 ans, la Ville de Vichy propose le passeport sportif. Pour une somme modique, il permet de pratiquer la VOILE, la PLANCHE A VOILE, le CANOE-KAYAK, la NATATION aux piscines d'été et d'hiver, le TENNIS, l'AVIRON, le TIR A L'ARC, le TIR A AIR COMPRIME et de bénéficier de conditions particulières pour le ski nautique, l'équitation et autres activités de plein-air.
- EQUITATION :
  - Centre équestre de Vichy : Le Vernet - Tél. (70) 98.24.76.
  - Poney-Club de Brughes : Bellerive - Tél. (70) 32.29.09.
- RANDONNEES A CHEVAL :
  - Gué Chervais : Cusset (10 km de Vichy) - Tél. (70) 41.80.40
  - Relais Jonon : Le Mayet-de-Montagne - Tél. (70) 56.40.59

loisirs

- COURSES DE CHEVAUX :
  Société des Courses : 11, rue Alquié - Tél. (70) 31.54.99
  - Meeting de trot : 20 réunions - 14 nocturnes (11 avec P.M.U.)
    Grand Prix du Conseil Municipal (juillet)
  - Meeting de galop : 15 réunions (4 avec P.M.U.)
    Grand Prix de la Ville de Vichy (fin juillet - début août)
- CONCOURS HIPPIQUE - Rue Jean-Jaurès
  - Epreuves d'élevage
  - Concours Hippique International de sauts d'obstacles (juin-juillet)
- COURSES DE LEVRIERS :
  Terrain du Concours Hippique (août)
- JEUX :
  - Grand Casino - Tél. (70) 31.68.88
    Boule - Roulette - Black Jack - Ecarté - Baccara - Banque ouverte
  - Elysée Palace - Tél. (70) 98.25.17 (ouvert toute l'année)
    Boule - Roulette - Baccara - Black Jack
- JEUX DE SOCIETES :
  Clubs de Bridge - Echecs - Scrabble - Billard
- 14 SALLES DE CINEMA
- CONCERTS DE PLEIN AIR
- FESTIVALS :
  Musique militaire - Majorettes - Fêtes nautiques
  Corridas (mi-août)
  Feux d'Artifice (14 juillet - 15 août) - Folklore
- GOLF MINIATURE & CANOTAGE :
  sur le Plan d'Eau
- PROMENADES EN BATEAUX :
  - Pierre Coulon - et - Louis Napoléon -
- BAC « Le Cygne » :
  Traversée de l'Allier (hauteur de la Rotonde)
- EXCURSIONS EN AUTOCARS :
  Vichy et l'Auvergne - T.P.N. : Place V. Hugo - Tél. (70) 32.05.31
- PARC D'ENFANTS - PARC DU SOLEIL
  Avenue de France - Tél. (70) 32.32.84
- POUR VOUS DISTRAIRE :
  Nombreux Night-Clubs, Cabarets et Discothèques
- VOUS APPRECIEREZ LES NOMBREUSES BONNES TABLES DE VICHY
  Ambiance et cadre sympathiques

culture

- GRAND CASINO :
  Tél. (70) 31.68.88
  14 Concerts - Récitals - Ballets - Shows - Variétés
  Théâtre - Conférences - Opéras
- ELYSEE-PALACE :
  Tél. (70) 98.25.17 (ouvert toute l'année)
  Chansonniers - Music-Hall - Revues - Opérettes - Conférences
- CENTRE CULTUREL VALERY-LARBAUD :
  15, rue Mal-Foch - Tél. (70) 32.15.33 (ouvert toute l'année)
  Connaissance du Monde - Alliance Française - Arts Bourbonnais
  Théâtres - Concours National d'Art Lyrique - Concerts
  Expositions - Peinture - Sculpture, etc.
- ACADEMIE INTERNATIONALE DE MUSIQUE :
  Stage de 4 semaines en août
  Centre Culturel Valery-Larbaud - Tél. (70) 32.15.33
- INSTITUT CULTUREL INTERNATIONAL :
  14, rue Maréchal-Foch
- MAISON DES JEUNES :
  Tél. (70) 32.04.68 (ouverte toute l'année)
  Théâtre - Concerts - Récitals - Conférences - Ateliers - Expositions
- BIBLIOTHEQUES :
  - Bibliothèque municipale
  - Bibliothèque Pour Tous
- MUSEES :
  - Chastel Franc - Boulevard Président-Kennedy
  - Musée de la Maison du Missionnaire - 18, avenue Thermale
- CENTRE DE RECHERCHES ARCHEOLOGIQUES DE VICHY ET SA REGION :
  2, rue Porte-de-France - Tél. (70) 98.98.11
- SOCIETE D'HISTOIRE ET D'ARCHEOLOGIE DE VICHY
- NOMBREUSES GALERIES DE PEINTURE

Writing and posting letters

BRIGHOUSE
HIGH SCHOOL
MODERN LANGUAGES
DEPARTMENT

Now you will learn how to purchase postage stamps in order to send letters and postcards home. You will also be shown how to write a letter in French, either to someone you know or to a hotel or campsite in order to reserve accommodation.

You'll need to know what kind of stamp to buy.

Here's what to say:

> *Je voudrais un timbre pour une lettre (une carte postale) pour l'Angleterre, s'il vous plaît.*

Once you know what stamp to buy, say:

> *Un timbre à ...... s'il vous plaît.*

The price goes in the space.

A
j'écoute

You'll now hear ten people buying stamps of various values. In your exercise book, note down how many stamps of each value are being bought.

6

Post offices
have signs
above each
section of the
counter to tell
you what you
can buy there.

If you want stamps, you must look for the sign: *Affranchissements*
You should be able to see it in the top right corner of this photo.

je révise
je révise
je révise

You'll need to know French numbers well to get the value of the stamp you
want, to understand how much you're being asked for and to say what
phone number you want when you're phoning home. So this is a good time
to look at the numbers again. Here are the key numbers from 1–1000.
Wherever you see **etc**., this means that the numbers follow on logically from
that point until the next change.

0 *zéro*	11 *onze*	21 *vingt et un*	71 *soixante et onze*
1 *un/une*	12 *douze*	22 *vingt-deux*	72 *soixante-douze*
2 *deux*	13 *treize*	etc.	73 *soixante-treize*
3 *trois*	14 *quatorze*	30 *trente*	etc.
4 *quatre*	15 *quinze*	31 *trente et un*	77 *soixante-dix-sept*
5 *cinq*	16 *seize*	32 *trente-deux*	78 *soixante-dix-huit*
6 *six*	17 *dix-sept*	etc.	79 *soixante-dix-neuf*
7 *sept*	18 *dix-huit*	40 *quarante*	80 *quatre-vingts*
8 *huit*	19 *dix-neuf*	50 *cinquante*	81 *quatre-vingt-un*
9 *neuf*	20 *vingt*	60 *soixante*	82 *quatre-vingt-deux*
10 *dix*		70 *soixante-dix*	90 *quatre-vingt-dix*

  91 *quatre-vingt-onze*
  92 *quatre-vingt-douze*
    etc.
  99 *quatre-vingt-dix-neuf*
100 *cent*
200 *deux cents*
300 *trois cents*
584 *cinq cent quatre-vingt-quatre*
999 *neuf cent quatre-vingt-dix-neuf*
1000 *mille*

Work in pairs. One of you should look at **this** page and the other at page 164.

You are the counter assistant in a post office; it is a very busy post office, and this is the rush hour! You have a queue of people waiting behind someone who has come in from a local firm with a pile of mail … your job now is to serve him or her courteously and efficiently … but quickly, too! The customer will tell you what she or he wants to post. Check how much each item costs and note the information down in your exercise book so that you can present a bill to the customer at the end. The employee worked out the cost before she or he left the office so you'd better be right!

	cartes	lettres	paquets 500g
France	1F 90	courrier lent 1F 90 courrier rapide 2F 20	10F 30
Europe	Communautaire (sauf Angl.) 1F 90 Angleterre 2F 50	Communautaire (sauf Angl.) 2F 20 Angleterre 2F 70	Communautaire (sauf Angl.) 12F 20 Angleterre 15F
États-Unis	6F	6F	35F

When you finish, turn to page 164 and play the other part.

+ *plus*   − *moins*   x *fois*   : *divisé par*   = *font*

For fun, and to practise the numbers, try giving each other sums to do in French.
Use the French words above to do sums like these:

a	4 + 7 =	f	14 : 2 =	k	48 − 15 =	p	26 : 13 =
b	13 + 9 =	g	65 x 2 =	l	36 − 4 =	q	8 x 8 =
c	30 : 5 =	h	45 : 7 =	m	48 x 2 =	r	16 : 16 =
d	14 x 3 =	i	22 x 5 =	n	36 : 12 =	s	19 x 3 =
e	27 : 9 =	j	62 − 8 =	o	85 : 5 =	t	10 − 10 =

*Il y a dix ans, le téléphone était
très mauvais en France.
Récemment on a changé le
système. Maintenant il est très
moderne et très rapide.*

Il y a – ago
était – was
on a changé – they changed
maintenant – now

How would you use this telephone?

Can you decide why there are two openings in this letter box?

To phone home when you're in France, dial 19.44…
and then your number as you would dial it normally but **without** the first 0.

Here's an example: normally for London you dial 01.123.4567
from France you dial 19.44   1.123.4567

The French say telephone numbers in groups of two or three figures.
For example, 54. 25. 03 would be said: *cinquante-quatre, vingt-cinq, zéro trois.*

Le courrier

There are really only two main occasions when you may need to be able to **write** in French. The first is when you have to leave a brief note for a French friend, perhaps after taking a phone message. The second is when you write a letter.

This might be a letter to a friend, or it might be a business letter, when you write to a hotel, a campsite or a tourist office, when you need to reserve a place to stay, or get information about a town or region you're going to visit.

j'apprends

What you write in the letter will depend on why you're writing, but here are some expressions which you may find useful when writing to someone you know. You would do well to learn them by heart:

Chère	Dear… (to a girl or a woman)
Cher	Dear… (to a boy or a man)
Je te remercie de ta lettre	Thank you for your letter
que j'ai reçue…	which I received…
Est-ce que je peux…	May I…
Est-ce que tu peux…	Can you…
J'arrive le… à…	I arrive on… at…
Quand est-ce que tu vas arriver?	When are you going to arrive?
du…au…	from the… to the…

Remember that you'll use *tu* when writing to a friend or someone you know well.

When it comes to signing off, here are some possibilities:

à bientôt	'until soon'	
amitiés	'with friendship'	} with love from
grosses bises	'love'	
écris-moi vite	'write back soon'	

The French write their address on the back of the envelope like this:

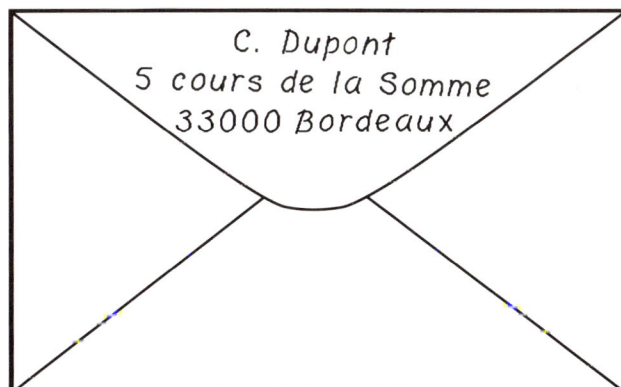

C. Dupont
5 cours de la Somme
33000 Bordeaux

Here's how to lay out both types of letter:

A letter to someone you know

the place and date
of writing

Paris le 20 Mai 1986

Cher Jean,
Je t'écris pour te demander de passer me voir lundi matin.
amitiés,
Georges

Dear John
(for a woman or
girl: *chère*)

amitiés is like
'love' in English

A business letter

the address of the people
to whom you are writing

Paris le 20 Mai 1986

16, rue Allat 98016 Paris

Editions AHno 155, bASt Michl PARIS 5e

your
address

Monsieur,
Je vous écris pour vous demander de m'envoyer la somme de 200,000 F d'ici 2 jours.
Je vous prie, Monsieur, d'agréer l'expression de mes sentiments distingués.

begin 'sir' and
not 'Dear Sir'

signing off

Londres, vendredi 2 mai.

Chère Anne,

je te remercie de ta lettre. J'espère arriver chez toi le 18 juin. J'arrive à la gare de Nantes à 15h30.

Est-ce que tu pourrais venir me rencontrer à la gare? J'ai hâte de te revoir!

A bientôt; amitiés.

Chantal

Hôtel Splendide
15-16 rue de la Paix
63000 Clermont-Ferrand

14 Main Street   le 2 mai
Church Stretton

Monsieur,

   J'ai l'intention de passer
deux jours à Clermond-Ferrand du 20
au 21 juin.
   Pourriez-vous me réserver une
chambre avec un grand lit et une
douche?

Je vous prie, Monsieur, d'accepter
l'expression de mes sentiments
distingués,

Your business letter should end with this rather flowery expression:

> *Je vous prie, Monsieur, d'accepter l'expression de mes sentiments distingués.*

All this means is 'Yours sincerely' or 'Yours faithfully'. Try to learn to write this out!
Without looking at the expression, try to write out the expression in your exercise book
using these blocks to remind you how many words it consists of.

j'apprends Here are some phrases which you may well find useful when writing a
business letter.

Je vous remercie de (votre lettre…)	Thank you for (your letter…)
J'ai l'intention de…	I intend to…
Je voudrais…	I would like…
du…au…	from the… to the…
Pourriez-vous (me réserver)	Could you (reserve me)
Avez-vous…	Have you…
Je compte rester…	I intend to stay…
J'aimerais avoir…	I would like to have…
Serait-il possible de…	Would it be possible to…
Suite à votre lettre du…	In reply to your letter of the…

If you find it really impossible to get *Je vous prie, Monsieur, d'accepter l'expression de
mes sentiments distingués* right, then use *sincèrement*. It's not as good but it'll do.

6

j'écoute

You will now hear ten dialogues in which various people ask for different things in a post office. Complete your copy of the chart below with the right answers:

	items wanted
1	
2	
3	
4	
5	
6	
7	
8	
9	
10	

Je voudrais des timbres

Je voudrais	un timbre
	deux timbres
		pour une lettre
		pour des lettres
		pour une carte
		  postale
		pour des cartes
		  postales
			pour l'Angleterre s'il vous plaît.

	un timbre à	un franc quarante deux francs vingt	

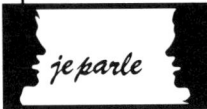

je parle   Work with your partner.

1 Ask for three stamps for letters home and two for cards.
2 Ask how to use the telephone. For practice, use your own phone number.
   (Je voudrais téléphoner, s'il vous plaît.)
3 Ask how much it costs to send a card home.
4 Send a letter to your French friend from the place in France where you are spending your holiday.
5 Send a letter and five cards home, or as many as you can for 6 francs 50. The letters are the most important items!

J'ai perdu...

You will have noticed that to say that something belongs to you, you need the words **mon, ma** and **mes**. All these three mean **my**, but which do you use?
If more than one thing is yours, you will use **mes**.

*J'ai perdu **mes** chaussures.*   I've lost my shoes.

Otherwise, you need to know whether the thing is a **le** word (**masculine**) or a **la** word (**feminine**).

*J'ai perdu **ma** cassette.*   I've lost my cassette.
*J'ai perdu **mon** passeport.*   I've lost my passport.

je parle

Practise saying that you have lost the items in this illustration, using *J'ai perdu* .

a   *mon sac*
b   *mon stylo*
c   *mon chapeau*
d   *mon cartable*
e   *ma canne*
f   *ma serviette*
g   *mon livre*
h   *mes lunettes*
i   *mon stylo*
j   *mon portefeuille*

If you lose something while you are in France, you will need to find the local *bureau des objets trouvés* (lost property office). The French name is much more optimistic than the English. It means 'found property office'!

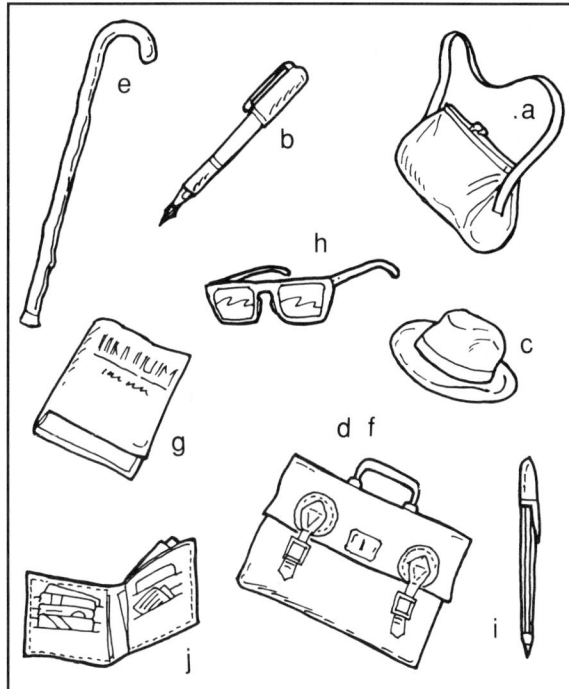

Où? When   *Quand?* When

Décrivez votre...... Describe your......

j'apprends

Here are some expressions which are useful when you want to say **when** something happened:

la semaine dernière	last week
mercredi dernier	last Wednesday
jeudi dernier	last Thursday
j'étais	I was
j'avais	I had
je l'avais	I had it

Here are some words which will help you **describe** whatever it is you have lost:

grand	big	*rouge*	red	*noir*	black	*marron*	brown
petit	small	*jaune*	yellow	*gris*	grey	*doré*	gold
large	wide	*bleu*	blue	*vert*	green	*argenté*	silver
lourd	heavy	*orange*	orange	*rose*	pink	*rayé*	striped
léger	light	*blanc*	white	*pourpre*	purple	*carré*	square
rond	round						

These phrases will help you say what the item is **made of**:

C'est en	*or.* *plastique.* *métal.* *argent.* *bois.*

It's made of	gold. plastic. metal. silver. wood.

Here is how to say **how big** something is:

Il *Elle*	*mesure environ.........* *centimètres.*

It measures about......... centimetres.

Here is **how much** it is worth:

Il *Elle*	*a une valeur d'environ.........* *francs.* *livres.*

It's worth about.........	francs. pounds.

Qu'est-ce qui s'est passé?

Qu'est-ce que vous avez perdu?	What have you lost?
Où l'avez-vous perdu?	Whereabouts did you lose it?

To answer this kind of question you will need to be able to talk about what has happened. Learn these phrases:

j'ai	I have
il a	he has
elle a	she has
on a	we have

Now you can use these expressions in the block diagrams below:

j'ai *il a* *elle a* *on a* *tu as* *vous avez*	*mangé* *regardé* *parlé* *perdu* *trouvé* *cherché* *rencontré* *vu* *bu* *pris* *mis*

I have he has she has we have you have you have	eaten watched spoken lost found looked for met seen drunk taken put

Using this you can say things like:

J'ai perdu mon manteau.	I've lost my coat.
Il a regardé Dallas.	He watched Dallas.

How to say you didn't do something

$$n' \ldots pas$$

je n'ai pas	mangé	I didn't	eat
il n'a pas	regardé	he didn't	look
elle n'a pas	trouvé	she didn't	find

See whether you understand these:

1 *Elle n'a pas regardé Dallas.*
2 *Il a cherché mon chien.*
3 *Je n'ai pas vu Pierre.*
4 *Elle a vu mon frère.*

You may want to compare this with the way **ne... pas** is used when you talk about what you **are not doing.** Look back to page 63 for this information.

je parle

1 Your neighbour can play the part of the official in the *bureau des objets trouvés.* You have lost your coat and you think you may have left it at the station. Describe it, and say roughly when you lost it.

2 Follow instructions as for no.1 only this time you've lost an expensive quartz watch *(une montre à quartz).*

3 Use the block diagrams on this and the previous page to say as much as possible about what you did yesterday.

Une dame est au guichet de la poste. Il n'y a pas beaucoup de monde. Elle va acheter des timbres.

le guichet – counter   *le monde* – people.

On va à la poste

Dialogue 1

Client	Bonjour Madame, je voudrais deux timbres à 3 francs 20, s'il vous plaît.
Agent des P et T	Voilà Monsieur… ça vous fait 6 francs 40, alors sur dix francs, je vous rends 3 francs 60.
Client	Merci bien, au revoir, Madame.
Agent des P et T	Au revoir, Monsieur.

Dialogue 2

Client	Bonjour Madame, je voudrais un timbre pour l'Angleterre, s'il vous plaît.
Agent des P et T	Oui, jeune homme. Pour une lettre ou pour une carte postale?
Client	Pour une lettre, s'il vous plaît.
Agent des P et T	Oui, alors cela vous fait 2 francs 20.

Dialogue 3

Cliente	Bonjour Monsieur, je voudrais téléphoner en Angleterre, s'il vous plaît.
Agent des P et T	Oui… alors prenez la cabine numéro deux… vous composez le 19, puis le 44… puis votre numéro.
Cliente	Merci Monsieur.

Dialogue 4

Cliente	Bonjour Monsieur, je voudrais deux timbres pour des lettres pour l'Angleterre.
Agent des P et T	Oui, Mademoiselle.
Cliente	Puis trois timbres pour des cartes postales pour l'Allemagne.
Agent des P et T	Bien Mademoiselle. Alors, cela vous fait 14 francs.
Cliente	Voilà.
Agent des P et T	Merci Mademoiselle.
Cliente	Merci Monsieur, au revoir.
Agent des P et T	Au revoir, Mademoiselle.

Agent des P et T (Agent des Postes at Télécommunications)

DIRECTIONS

AFFRANCHISSEMENTS

Télégrammes

GUICHET FERMÉ

Objets
recommandés
en
instance

**CABINES
TÉLÉPHONIQUES**

INSTANCES PAQUETS

INSTANCES LETTRES

À la maison

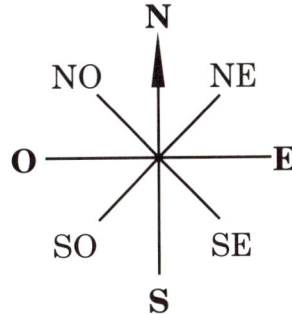

You may be asked about where you live:

Tu habites dans une maison ou en appartement? — Do you live in a house or a flat?
Comment est ta maison? — What is your house like?
Elle est grande, ta maison? — Is your house big?
Comment est ta ville? — What is your town like?
Il y a combien d'habitants à Oxford? — How many people live in Oxford?

Here are some phrases which should help you tackle this kind of question:

Ma maison est… — My house is…
Il y a… — There is /there are…
J'habite à Wolverhampton. — I live in Wolverhampton.
Il y a… habitants à… — There are … people living in…
J'habite dans une petite maison. — I live in a small house
C'est une grande/petite ville. — It is a large/small town.
Ma maison se trouve… — My house is located…
Bristol se trouve au sud-ouest de l'Angleterre. — Bristol is in south-west England.
Shrewsbury se trouve dans le Shropshire. — Shrewsbury is in Shropshire.
Bristol est à 121 km d'Exeter. — Bristol is 75 miles from Exeter.

je parle

With your partner, practise asking and answering any of these questions about where you live. Change the place names to suit yourselves.

*trois… D
deux…
un…TOP!*

Once again, you have a second or two in which to find some way of answering the question! This time, you are being asked about what has happened, or what you have done. Answer as fast as you can, before the bleep!

First your French family ask you about your trip to the nearby town, then your French correspondent's friends ask you about what you have been doing.

j'écris

1 Write your first letter to a French penfriend. Introduce yourself, talk about your likes, dislikes and interests. Ask your penfriend about her or his interests. Write the whole letter, starting it and signing off the way you've been shown. Aim to write about 60 words.

2 Write a letter to your French penfriend. Talk about your school. Say which subjects you like or dislike. Ask your penfriend about her or his school. Write the whole letter, starting it and signing off the way you've been shown. Aim to write about 60 words.

3 Write out the phrase used to sign off a formal letter, then check that you've got it right! If you've made a mistake, write it out again!

4 You receive this postcard from a French friend. When you go on holiday you too write a card. In this you should say what the weather is like, what you think of the place where you are staying and what you are doing there. Aim at about 30 words. Try not to copy too much from the card.

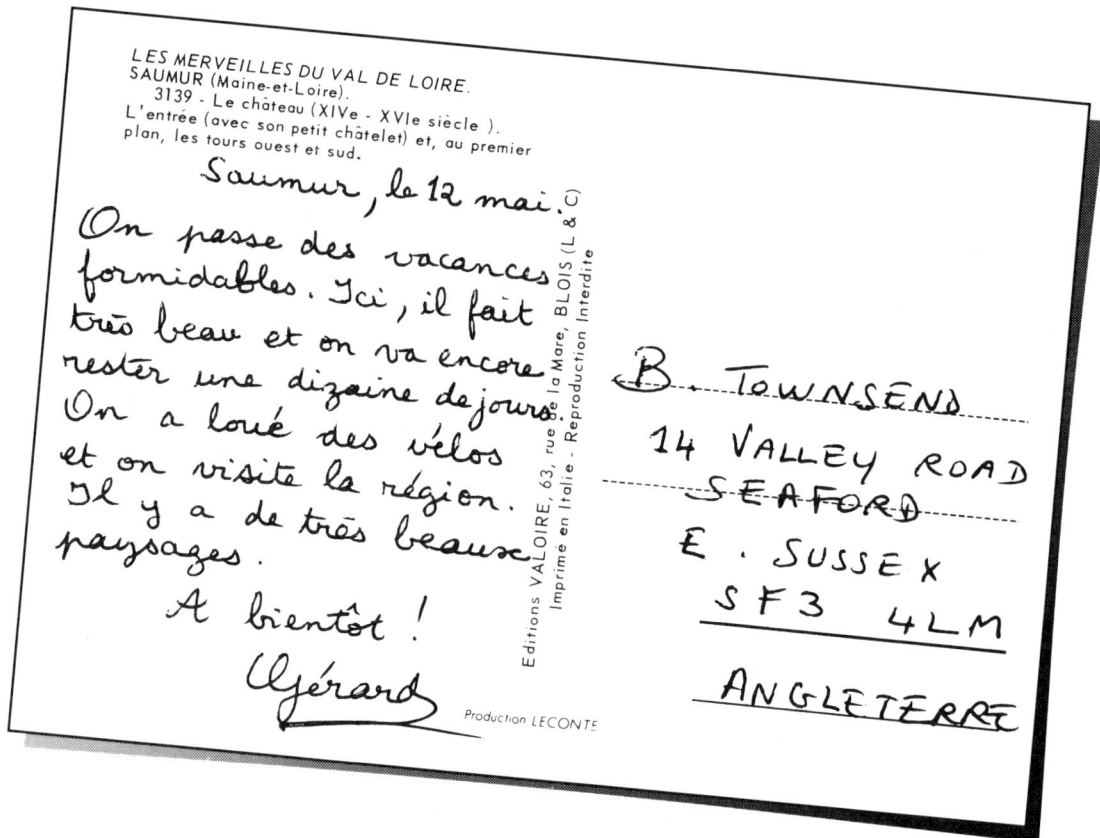

LES MERVEILLES DU VAL DE LOIRE.
SAUMUR (Maine-et-Loire).
3139 - Le château (XIVe - XVIe siècle).
L'entrée (avec son petit châtelet) et, au premier
plan, les tours ouest et sud.

Saumur, le 12 mai.

On passe des vacances formidables. Ici, il fait très beau et on va encore rester une dizaine de jours. On a loué des vélos et on visite la région. Il y a de très beaux paysages.

A bientôt !

Gérard

Editions VALOIRE, 63, rue de la Mare, BLOIS (L & C)
Imprimé en Italie - Reproduction Interdite

Production LECONTE

B. TOWNSEND
14 VALLEY ROAD
SEAFORD
E. SUSSEX
SF3 4LM
ANGLETERRE

5 Read this letter from a French friend. Answer the letter. Aim at about 60 words. Try not to copy too much from the letter.

> Nîmes, le 12 juin.
>
> Bonjour John,
> Je m'appelle Gérard.
> J'habite à quelques kilomètres de Nîmes.
> J'ai quinze ans et je suis fils unique.
> Mon père est agriculteur et ma mère l'aide
> dans son travail.
> J'aime beaucoup jouer au foot-ball, mais
> depuis l'année dernière, je fais aussi du
> judo.
>   Et toi ? Quel âge as-tu ?
> Est-ce que tu as des frères ou des soeurs ?
> Quelle est la profession de ton père ?
> Est-ce-que ta mère a aussi un travail ?
> Est-ce-que tu fais beaucoup de sport ?
>   J'espère recevoir bientôt de tes nouvelles.
>
> Amitiés.
>
> Gérard

6 Imagine that you are staying with your French penfriend, but that you have to go out soon. You are alone in the house when a French boy called Marc calls at the door. Write a note for your friend saying that Marc called round, and that he is going to come back at 8 o'clock.

Remember that your French does not have to be perfect, but you must get the message across somehow.

7 Write a letter to the Camping de Ribou near Cholet. You and your family would like to stay there for two nights during August. Find out whether there are showers and a shop on the site, and ask how much it will cost.

Ces enfants portent l'uniforme du collège! C'est à dire qu'il n'y a pas d'uniforme en France!

School in France is organised differently to English schools. Instead of first year, second year, etc., there are *classes*. They can be compared to our system like this:

English		French
VI	- - - - -	T
VI	- - - - -	1
5	- - - - -	2
4	- - - - -	3
3	- - - - -	4
2	- - - - -	5
1	- - - - -	6

In England, all you have to do to move from one year to the next is to get older! In France, you have to **earn** the right to move up into the next class; in other words, your work must reach a particular standard. If it does **not**, then you will have to do the same year again! This means that you get pupils of different ages in the same class. This *redoublement* (staying down a year) is not thought of as a punishment; it's really a way of helping a pupil to reach the standard required. If after a year the pupil still hasn't reached that standard, then she or he moves up anyway, as in this country.

Voici une classe d'anglais dans un CES (Collège d'Enseignement Secondaire) à Doué-la-Fontaine dans la vallée de la Loire. Le professeur explique quelque chose en anglais.

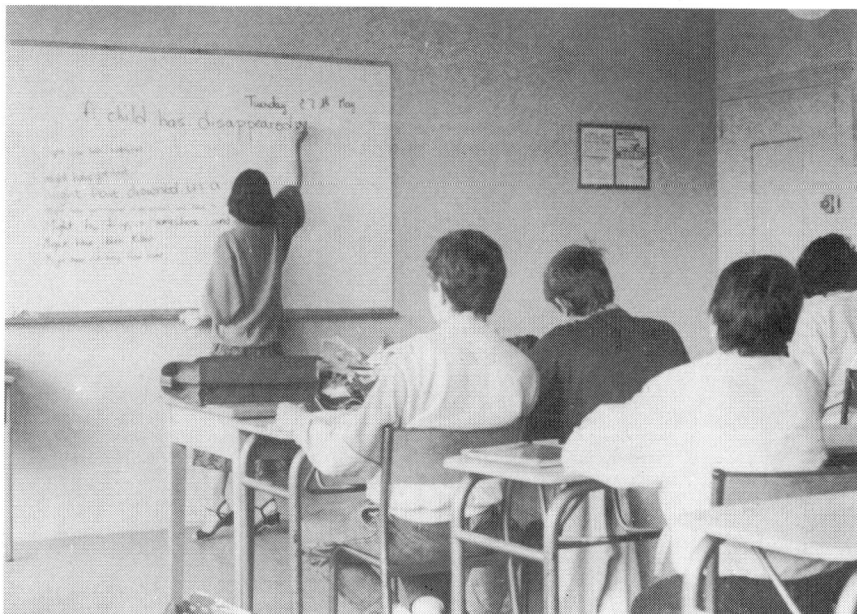

English is the first foreign language taught in French schools; German comes next, then Spanish, Italian, Russian and so on, although not all of these languages are taught in every school.

Cette fille va répondre à la question du professeur.
Elle aime bien l'anglais, sans doute.
En France, l'anglais est une matière importante, comme le français en Angleterre.

comme – like

Many schools are closed on Wednesday afternoons but open on Saturday mornings. This means that they can't travel far from the school at the weekend because it's too short.

Lessons are usually 50 minutes long and there is usually a break in the morning and in the afternoon, but school begins at 8h00 and ends at 17h00. On the other hand, the lunch hour can be from 12h00 until 14h00, and some lessons are free lessons. During free lessons pupils go into *permanence* (a sort of study lesson). This is supervised by a *surveillant* (usually a student) who is in charge of discipline outside the classroom.

Voici l'abri des vélos.
Certains élèves viennent au collège à vélo, d'autres en car ou en voiture.
Quelques-uns ont des mobylettes.

> *l'abri* – shelter
> *viennent* – come
> *quelques-uns* – some

Voici la cantine du CES Lucien Millet à Doué-la-Fontaine. Les élèves mangent ici, mais les professeurs mangent dans une salle à part.
La nourriture est très bonne.

> *ici* – here
> *à part* – separate
> *la nourriture* – food

RÉSUMÉ

Leçon 6

You should be able to:

1 find the stamp counter in a post office;
2 ask for a stamp for a letter or postcard;
3 use and recognise numbers and amounts of money;
4 phone home from France;
5 tackle simple letter-writing;
6 say you've lost something and describe it to an official in a lost property office;
7 talk about some things which have happened in the past;
8 leave a message for someone (see below).

Je laisse un message

If someone telephones or calls at your French friend's house while the French family are out, you may need to be able to leave a message for them.
This type of writing does not need to be in perfect French or full sentences, you just need to get the important details across. Here are some examples of messages, containing some useful expressions which you can use when you leave one.

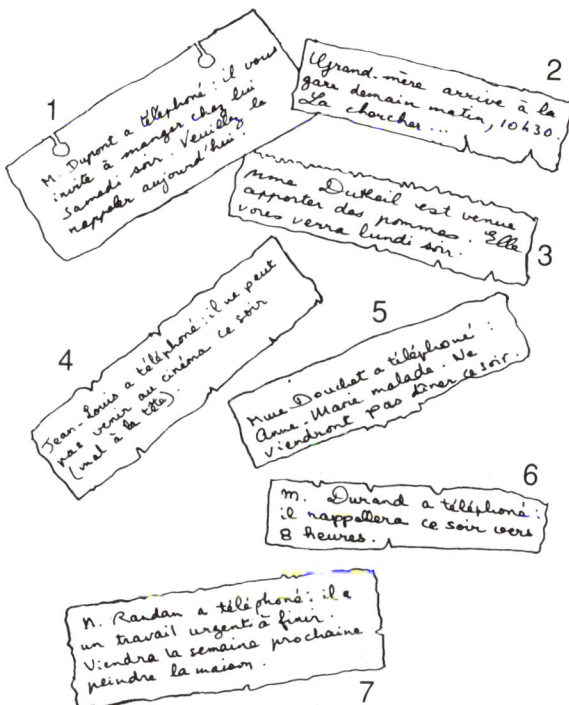

RÉPERTOIRE

À la poste

un timbre	stamp
une lettre	letter
une carte postale	postcard
affranchissements	stamps

Numéros

plus	plus
moins	less
divisé par	divided by
fois	times
font	equals

Lettres

à bientôt	until soon
amitiés	love
grosses bises	love
écris-moi vite	write soon
cher chère	} dear

Divers

j'ai	I have
où	where
quand	when
décrivez	describe
j'étais	I was
j'avais	I had

Descriptions

grand	big/tall
petit	small/short
large	wide
lourd	heavy
léger	light
rond	round
rayé	striped
carré	square
c'est en…	it's made of…

Matières

or	gold
plastique	plastic
métal	metal
argent	silver
bois	wood

Couleurs

rouge	red
jaune	yellow
bleu	blue
orange	orange
blanc	white
noir	black
gris	grey
vert	green
rose	pink
pourpre	purple
marron	brown
doré	golden
argenté	silver

At the railway station

Now you will learn how to buy tickets of various kinds and how to make a reservation. We will also look at how to use the 24-hour clock which is used in train timetables.

If you look at the picture on the left you will see the letters

SNCF

This stands for *Société Nationale des Chemins de Fer français* (the national society of French railways). Look for SNCF when you want to find the station. It is often used on road signs.

Voici l'extérieur de la gare de Cholet.
C'est une petite gare.   *Et voici le guichet.*

DIRECTIONS

Do you recognise these station signs?

ARRIVÉES

Buffet

CAFÉ

TOILETTES

Consigne

Kiosque à journaux

DÉPARTS

restaurant

TÉLÉPHONES

accès aux quais

Composter vos billets

BILLETS

16 33

```
                    DEPART
      ANGERS                        NANTES
   6 H 29  SANS CORRESPONDANCE POUR PARIS LES DF    6 H 37  SAUF DF
   7 H 53                          7 H 26  SAUF DF
 O 10 H 06  SAUF DF                8 H 43
   13 H 42                         10 H 14  CAR  DIRECT NANTES
 O 17 H 19  SAUF DF  SANS CORRESPONDANCE POUR PARIS LES SAMEDIS  13 H 05
   18 H 05  DF  TRAIN DIRECT PARIS MP   16 H 36  SAUF DF
   18 H 37  SAUF DF                18 H 20  SAUF DF
   19 H 42  DF                     20 H 42  DF
   22 H 19  SAUF SAMEDIS
                                      PARTHENAY
                                         CARS
                                   5 H 55  SAUF SAMEDIS  DF
  O : TRAIN  AVEC SUPPLEMENT D'ANGERS A PARIS MP   16 H 25  SAUF SAMEDI
  D F : DIMANCHES ET FETES         18 H 35  POITIERS
```

```
                    ARRIVEE
      ANGERS                        NANTES
   7 H 48  SAUF SAMEDIS ET DF     8 H 35  SAUF DF
   10 H 00                        9 H 44  SAUF DF
   12 H 45                        13 H 01
   15 H 00  SAUF DF               18 H 08  SAUF DF
   17 H 18                        18 H 33  CAR
   19 H 19  SAUF DF               19 H 37  DF
   19 H 32  DF                    19 H 45  SAUF DF
   20 H 05  VENDREDIS
   20 H 44  SAUF VENDREDIS ET DF     PARTHENAY
   20 H 58  DF                         CARS
   22 H 05  VENDREDIS           9 H 44  SAUF SAMEDIS  DF
   23 H 00                      10 H 12  DE POITIERS
                                20 H 17  SAUF SAMEDI
  DF : DIMANCHES ET FETES
```

je travaille

Write answers to these questions in your excercise book.

1 Which are the two large towns to which you can go directly by train?
2 How would you get to Parthenay?
3 What does *O* mean on the departures board?
4 What does *DF* mean on the departures board?
5 When does the last train arrrive from Nantes on Sunday?
6 When does the fastest train for Paris leave?
7 Why is this the quickest way to get to Paris?
8 Looking at these boards, would you say this was a busy station (give reasons)?
9 What does the word *correspondance* mean?
10 What does the word *sauf* mean?

je révise je révise je révise

de from	*pour* to

When asking for information about trains, don't forget that these two words, however small they may seem, make a big difference.

> *À quelle heure arrive le train **pour** Dieppe?*
> When does the train **to** Dieppe arrive?

> *À quelle heure arrive le train **de** Dieppe?*
> When does the train **from** Dieppe arrive?

In station announcements, they make things clear by using these expressions:

> *Le train à destination de…*   The train to…
> *Le train en provenance de…*   The train from…

À la gare

You'll notice that French railway platforms are very low, so low that you have to climb up into the train. The trains have special mini-steps which fold away when you close the door.

There are two important words to remember, *le quai* (which is the platform between two tracks) and *la voie* (which is the track). Mix these two up and you may find yourself on the wrong train.

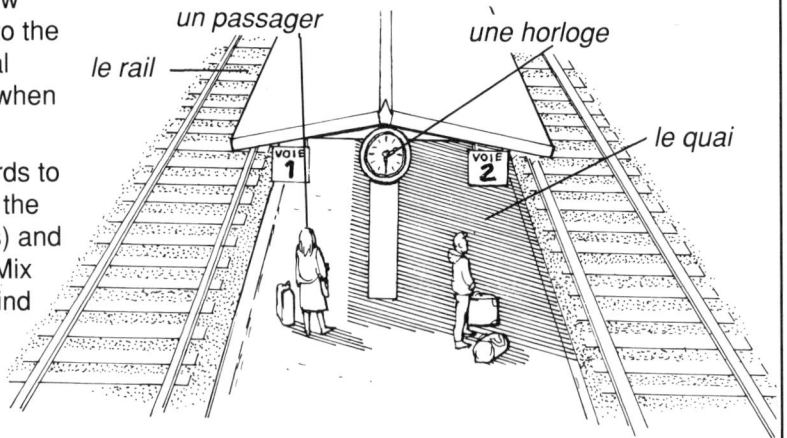

un passager

le rail

une horloge

le quai

VOIE 1

VOIE 2

Réservations

It is often sensible to make a reservation. In the summer, French trains can be extremely crowded, and you may well find yourself sitting on your suitcase in the corridor for many hours! Don't forget that France is a large country (more than twice the area of England, Wales and Scotland put together) which means that journey times tend to be longer than in this country.

Suppléments

Watch what train you get on (even if it's going the right way!) If you get on some express trains, you could easily find yourself paying an excess charge.

La gare de Cholet. Il fait beau. Un train arrive: c'est un autorail. Ces trains sont rouges et blancs. Ils s'appellent parfois des Michelines et ne sont pas très rapides.

Expressions utiles

il y a can mean either **there is** or **there are**
y a-t-il can mean either **is there?** or **are there?**

Y a-t-il un train pour Bordeaux aujourd'hui, s'il vous plaît?
Y a-t-il une cabine téléphonique près d'ici, s'il vous plaît?

Il y a un train à 13h30, Monsieur?
Il y a une cabine dans le foyer, Madame?

How to buy tickets and make reservations

When buying a ticket, you'll want to be able to choose between a single *(un aller simple)* and a return *(un aller et retour)*, between a first class ticket and a second class ticket *(en première, en deuxième classe)*.

Je voudrais	un aller simple, un aller et retour,	s'il vous plaît.

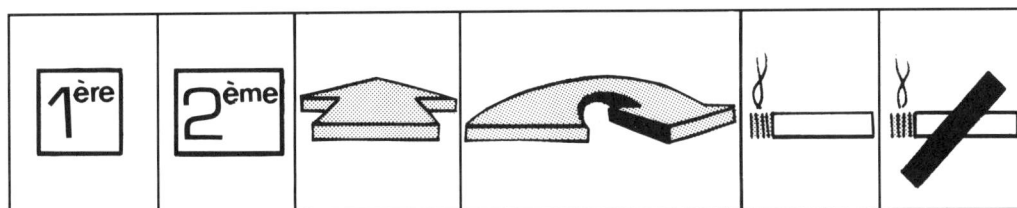

| en première classe | en deuxième classe | un aller simple | un aller et retour | un compartiment pour fumeurs | un compartiment pour non-fumeurs |

Voici une Micheline rouge et blanche!

À quelle heure...?

Most timetables use the 24 hour clock, of course, as they do in this country:

Le train de Paris arrive à 21h10.
Le vol No. 245 à destination de Londres part à 18h30.

With your partner, practise reading these digital-style clock faces:

| 12:50 | 13:12 | 16:20 | 18:15 | 08:10 |
| 20:05 | 00:05 | 14:25 | 11:26 | 21:39 |

je parle

With your partner playing the part of a French railway official, try the following exercises:

1 Buy a return ticket to Lyon (2nd class).
2 Get a reserved seat on the 23h10 train to Paris *(Gare du Nord)*
3 Ask when the Bordeaux train leaves.
4 Buy a single ticket to Calais. Travel in style; get a first class ticket. Make sure you get a non-smoker's compartment.
5 Ask on which platform the train for Lyon is standing.

j'écoute **A**

You will now hear a series of ten people asking for various things, either at the ticket office or at the reservations counter. Complete your copy of the chart below to show that you have understood the conversations.

	passenger's destination	single or return	type of compartment	cost
1				
2				
3				
4				
5				
6				
7				
8				
9				
10				

First, second, third…

On page 55 you learned the words for first, second and third. You may need others like this. They are not difficult to put together. Usually, you just take the number you want and add **-ième**. For example, with six you add **-ième** and this gives you *sixième.*

A few numbers get odd letters added or dropped: these are <u>underlined</u> below. Here are more examples:

1 *premier/première* (in English a première is the **first** showing of a film)

2 *deuxième*	6 *sixième*	10 *dixième*	14 *quator<u>z</u>ième*	18 *dix-huitième*
3 *troisième*	7 *septième*	11 *on<u>z</u>ième*	15 *quin<u>z</u>ième*	19 *dix-neu<u>v</u>ième*
4 *quat<u>r</u>ième*	8 *huitième*	12 *dou<u>z</u>ième*	16 *sei<u>z</u>ième*	20 *vingtième*
5 *cin<u>qu</u>ième*	9 *neu<u>v</u>ième*	13 *trei<u>z</u>ième*	17 *dix-septième*	

*je révise
je révise
je révise*

Je voudrais…

You probably remember *Je voudrais* means 'I would like'. When you are asking for something, you usually have to use *de la* or *de* as well. Do a bit of detective work on the following sentences to see if you can figure out when to use *de la* and when you use *du:*

1 *Je voudrais du savon, s'il vous plaît.*	*le savon* – soap
2 *Je voudrais du chocolat, s'il vous plaît.*	*le chocolat* – chocolate
3 *Je voudrais de la confiture, s'il vous plaît.*	*la confiture* – jam
4 *Je voudrais de la farine, s'il vous plaît.*	*la farine* – flour
5 *Je voudrais de la margarine, s'il vous plaît.*	*la margarine* – margarine
6 *Je voudrais du beurre, s'il vous plaît.*	*le beurre* – butter
7 *Je voudrais de la limonade, s'il vous plaît.*	*la limonade* – lemonade
8 *Je voudrais du lait, s'il vous plaît.*	*le lait* – milk
9 *Je voudrais du sel, s'il vous plaît.*	*le sel* – salt
10 *Je voudrais de la bière, s'il vous plaît.*	*la bière* – beer

If you think you know how this works, try asking for these things:

la lessive – washing powder	*le thé* – tea
le jus d'orange – orange juice	*la sauce* – sauce or gravy
le café – coffee	*le bois* – wood
la menthe – mint	*le fromage* – cheese
le gâteau – cake	*le pâté* – pâté

If you're still unsure ask your teacher.

Quick quiz

Can you guess the meanings of these eight SNCF signs?

Answer on page 101.

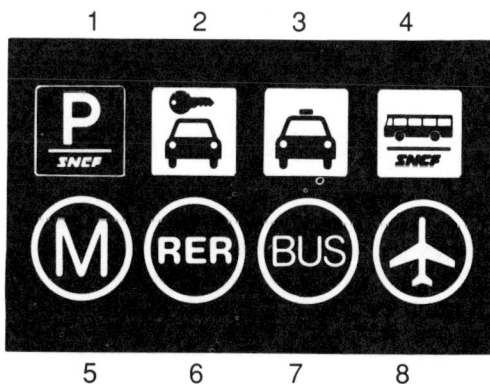

JEU DE RÔLES

Work in pairs. One of you should look at **this** page and the other at page 165.

You are playing the parts of six passengers who are about to travel by train. Each passenger is beginning her or his journey from one of the main line stations in Paris.

In the boxes below you will see where each passenger wants to go, together with other details of the kind of ticket and reservation required.

Your partner is the ticket salesperson, and then the official at the reservations counter! In each case, after buying your ticket and reserving a seat, find out **when** and **from which platform** the next train leaves. Ask any other questions given in the box.

When you finish, turn to page 165 and play the other part.

LYON

1ère

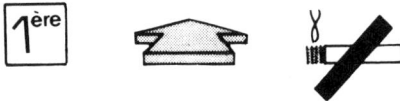

Ask if there are other trains for Lyon between now (it's midday) and 6pm.

LONDRES

2ème

Ask if there is a restaurant car on the train *(un wagon-restaurant)*.

AMIENS

2ème

Ask if you have to change trains. *(Est-ce qu'il faut changer?)*

BORDEAUX

2ème

Ask if there is a restaurant car on the train *(un wagon-restaurant)*.

ANNECY

1ère

Ask when the next train leaves (i.e. after the one the assistant tells you about).

RENNES

2ème

Ask what time the train arrives in Bordeaux.
(À quelle heure est-ce que le train arrive…)

À quelle heure part le train?

Dialogue 1

Client	Bonjour, Madame.
Employée	Bonjour, Monsieur.
Client	Un aller et retour pour Paris, s'il vous plaît.
Employée	Oui, Monsieur…en deuxième classe?
Client	Oui…
Employée	Ça vous fait 80 francs.
Client	Voilà. Est-ce que je peux réserver?
Employée	Oui…là-bas sur votre gauche, Monsieur.

Dialogue 2

Client	Je voudrais réserver une place dans le train de 21 heures 30 pour Paris, s'il vous plaît.
Employée	Oui, Monsieur. Montrez-moi votre billet, s'il vous plaît.
Client	Voilà.
Employée	Merci…vous voulez un compartiment fumeurs?
Client	Non merci.
Employée	Alors, voici votre billet. Cela vous fait 15 francs.

Dialogue 3

Passagère	Pardon, Monsieur. À quelle heure part le train pour Rouen, s'il vous plaît?
Contrôleur	Il part à 18 heures, Madame.
Passagère	Et de quel quai, Monsieur?
Contrôleur	Du quai numéro trois, Madame.
Passagère	Merci bien, Monsieur.
Contrôleur	De rien, Madame.

Dialogue 4

Une dame	Pardon Monsieur, à quelle heure arrive le train de Dieppe?
Employé	Le train de Dieppe? Il arrive à seize heures vingt, Madame, au quai numéro un.
Une dame	Merci bien, Monsieur.

trois... C
deux...
un...TOP!

Once again, you have a second or two in which to find some way of answering the question! You are at the railway station buying a ticket and making a reservation. Answer as fast as you can before the bleep!

j'écris

1 Imagine that your class is linked with one in a French CES. As part of a package of material being sent to the French school you have been asked to write a description of your daily routine. Aim at about 60 words, begin with breakfast time and talk about a typical day, either during the week or at the weekend.

2 Imagine that you are staying with your French penfriend. You are alone in the house when the phone rings. Write a note for your friend's parents saying that Monsieur Vérien rang, that he can't go to the restaurant with them this evening because his wife is ill. He will ring again tomorrow.

Remember that your French does not have to be perfect, but you must get the message across somehow.

3 Write a letter to the tourist office in Orange. You and your family would like to spend a week in July. Get them to send you information about the town, hotels, things to visit, entertainment and so on.

4 Your French friend sends you the following postcard. When you go on holiday to Blackpool you send a postcard to your friend in reply. Write that postcard. Don't use too much of the material in this card.

BASILIQUE du SACRE COEUR
de MONTMARTRE
Mosaïques
· « LYNACOLOR » ·

Paris, le 25 juillet

Je suis arrivé à Paris il y a trois jours. Il fait beau. Je prends souvent le bus et je vais voir les monuments. Hier, j'ai visité le musée du Louvre

Amitiés

Patrice

ABEILLE-CARTES - Editions LYNA-PARIS
8, rue du Caire, 75002 PARIS - Tel. 236.41.28
Reproduction interdite.

L. MERSON
3 Butcher's row
ALSAGER
STAFFORDSHIRE
AL 3 6 NJ

ANGLETERRE

2

Couleurs Naturelles

Il y a six chaînes de télévision en France.

TF1 (Télévision Française 1) est une chaîne privée, et il y a beaucoup de publicité sur cette chaîne. **A2 (Antenne 2)** correspond à peu près à BBC1 en Angleterre. Il y a beaucoup d'émissions d'informations, par exemple.

FR3 (France Régionale 3) est une chaîne où la culture est un peu plus importante. Dans la journée elle donne des émissions régionales. Le soir elle passe beaucoup de films.

Canal Plus est une chaîne un peu spéciale – on a besoin d'un décodeur. Le code change tous les mois. On y passe beaucoup de films et d'émissions de sport.

La 5 présente surtout des feuilletons ou des séries comme 'Star Trek' et 'Knight Rider' et souvent ils sont répétés trois fois dans la même journée.

M6 s'adresse aux jeunes. Elle passe beaucoup de vidéoclips de chanteurs de musique pop, mais elle passe aussi des films et des séries.

la chaîne – channel	*à peu près* – roughly
une émission – programme	*il y a* – there are
les informations – news	*donne* – puts on
le décodeur – decoding device	*passent* – are put on
le feuilleton – soap opera or series	*on a besoin de* – you need
le vidéoclip – video (pop video)	*comme* – like
a été – was	*tous les mois* – every month
surtout – mainly	*s'adresse aux* – is aimed at

MERCREDI 4 MARS

TELEVISION FRANÇAISE I
8h30 : La une chez vous. — 8h45 : Salut les petits loups. — 11h30 : La séquence du spectateur. — 12h : Tournez manège. — 13h : Journal. — 14h45 : Cœur de diamant. — 15h15 — 15h15 : Vitamine. — 17h30 : La vie des bêtes. — 18h : Huit çà suffit. — 18h25 : Journal. — 18h45 : La roue de la fortune. — 19h10 : Santa Barbara. — 19h40 : Cocoricocoboy. — 20h : Journal. — 20h35 : Strip Tease. — 21h35 : Les sciences et la vie. — 23h : Une dernière. — 23h25 : Premier plan.

ANTENNE 2
6h45 : Télématin. — 8h30 : Jeunes docteurs pour la vie. — 9h : Récré A2. — 12h05 : L'académie des 9. — 13h : Journal. — 13h45 : Michel Strogoff. — 14h40 : Terre des bêtes. — 15h : Récré A2. — 17h45 : Mambo satin. — 18h05 : Madame est servie. — 18h30 : C'est la vie. — 18h50 : Des chiffres et des lettres. — 19h15 : Actualités régionales. — 19h40 : Le théâtre de Bouvard. — 20h : Journal. — 20h30 : « Un train dans la nuit », téléfilm de Igor Auzins, avec Hugh Keas-Byrne, Ingrid Mason, Max Meldrum. — 22h05 : Moi je... — 23h05 : Journal.

FRANCE REGIONS 3
14h : Splendeur sauvage. — 14h30 : Cameraventure. — 15h : Agatha Christie. — 15h50 : Jazz off. — 16h : Des chercheurs pour qui. — 17h : Demain l'amour. — 17h25 : Jeunesse. — 19h15 : Actualités régionales. — 19h55 : Dessin animé. — 20h05 : La classe. — 20h35 : La nouvelle affiche. — 21h55 : Thalassa. — 22h45 : Soir 3. — 23h15 : Bal masqué chez les Rohan.

FILMS PROGRAMMES SUR CANAL PLUS
(Les heures de passages correspondent aux jours indiqués)
Pouvoir intime, film policier canadien d'Yves Simoneau (1986), avec Marie Tifo, Pierre Curzi, Jacques Godin. **Mer. 4 à 8h45.**
Shampoo, comédie américaine de Hal Hahby (1975), avec Goldie Hawn, Warren Beatty, Julie Christie, Lee Grant, Jack Waerden. **Mer. 4 à 10h10, ven. 6 à 23h, dim. 8 à 22h15, lun 9 à 20h35.**
Guerre et passion, film d'aventure anglais de Peter Hyams (1979), avec Lesley-Anne Down, Christopher Plummer, Harrison Ford. **Mer. 4 à 21h, sam. 7 à 8h45.**

LA CINQ
SERIES ET FEUILLETONS
Princesse Sarah, t.l.j. à 7h00, 17h10.
Arnold et Willy, t.l.j. à 7h50 et 17h45.
Happy days, t.l.j. à 8h15, 19h05.
Star trek, t.l.j. à 8h45, 14h15.
Chips, mer. 4, sam. 7, mar. 10 à 9h45, jeu. 5 à 16h, ven. 7 à 9h45 et 16h, lun. 9 à 16h.
Jaimie, t.l.j. à 10h30 et 18h15.
Mission impossible, t.l.j. (sf dim.) à 11h30 et 19h35, dim. 8 à 19h35.
Supercopter, mer. 4 à 12h25, jeu. 5 à 15h05, ven. 6 à 12h25 et 15h05, sam. 7 à 12h25, lun. 9 à 15h05, mar. 10 à 12h25 et 16h.

TV 6
Alice dans les villes, film allemand de Wim Wenders (1973), avec Rudiger Vogler, Yella Rottlander, Elisabeth Kreuser, ven. 27 à 20h30.
Le vampire de ces dames, film américain de Stan Dragoti (1979), avec George Hamilton, Susan Saint-Georges, lun. 9 à 20h30.
Le souffle de la tempête, film américain de Alan J. Pakula (1978), avec James Caan, Jane Fonda, Jason Robards, mar. 10 à 20h30.

You should be able to:

1 recognise common railway station signs;
2 read the arrivals and departures boards
3 buy a ticket at a station and make a reservation, deciding whether you want a single, a return, a first or second-class compartment and a smokers' or non-smokers' compartment;
4 tell the time in French using the 24-hour clock;
5 ask if there's a train for a particular town and understand the reply;
6 say you'd like something.

RÉPERTOIRE

À la gare

arrivées	arrivals
départs	departures
buffet	buffet
café	café
consigne	left luggage
kiosque	kiosk
accès aux quais	to the platforms
composter	to stamp
un billet	a ticket
un guichet	a ticket office
correspondance	connection
un quai	island platform
une voie	a track
un rail	a rail
une horloge	a clock
un autorail	a railcar
un compartiment	a compartment

je travaille

1 If you wanted to get from the main station at Lyon, Lyon Perrache, to Paris by about seven in the evening, what trains could you take?
2 Try to work out what notes 1, 3, 4 and 6 mean.

Numéro du train		618	736	7166	7416/7	5624	5156/7	24	5046	670	924	5052	622	713/2	624	5050	626	740	386	5903/2
Notes à consulter		1	2		3	4	5	6	7	8	9	10	11	12	13	14	15	16	17	
		X																		
Lyon-Perrache	D	11.46								13.20		13.36	13.48		14.49		15.46			
Lyon-Part-Dieu	D	12.00	12.00			12.49				13.30		13.45	14.00	14.00	15.00	14.57	16.00	16.00		
Villefranche-sur-Saone	D											14.05								
Macon-Loché-TGV	D										14.50									
Macon-Ville	D					13.28						14.32				15.35				
Tournus	D											14.49								
Chalon-sur-Saone	D			12.25		13.59						15.04					16.06		16.10	
Chagny	D			12.46	13.10							15.15							16.36	17.03
Beaune	D			13.02	13.24							15.25								17.17
Dijon-Ville	A			13.40	13.47	14.00	14.33	14.43	14.51			15.45				16.40				17.39
Montbard	A								15.27			16.40								
Laroche-Migennes	A								16.15			17.28				17.59				
Paris-Gare-de-Lyon	A	14.04	14.04			16.47		16.23	18.06	15.34	16.34	18.56	16.04	16.04	17.04	19.16	18.00	18.00		

Les trains circulant tous les jours ont leurs horaires indiqués en gras.
Tous les trains offrent des places assises en 1re et 2e cl. sauf indication contraire dans les notes.

X Train n'offrant pas la totalité de ses prestations sur tout son parcours ou sur toute sa circulation.

Notes :

1. Ne prend pas de voyageurs pour Lyon-Part-Dieu. A supplément certains jours. TGV.

2. A supplément certains jours. TGV.

3. Circule tous les jours sauf les dim et fêtes.

4. Circule les 27, 28 déc 86, 4, 5 jan, 21, 22 et 28 fév 87.

5. CORAIL.

6. A supplément certains jours. TGV. 2e CL.

7. Circule les dim sauf les 9 nov 86 et 19 avr 87;Circule les 11 nov 86 et 20 avr 87.

8. Circulation périodique.Renseignez-vous. Ne prend pas de voyageurs pour Lyon-Part-Dieu. TGV.

9. TGV. 2e CL.

10. CORAIL. certains jours.

11. Circule tous les jours sauf les 19 avr, 2 et 9 mai 87. Ne prend pas de voyageurs pour Lyon-Part-Dieu. TGV.

12. Circule tous les jours sauf les 19 avr, 2 et 9 mai 87. TGV.

13. Ne prend pas de voyageurs pour Lyon-Part-Dieu. TGV.

14. CORAIL.

Nota : A Paris-Gare-de-Lyon, l'office de tourisme de Paris assure un service d'information touristique et de réservation hôtelière.

Taking the car to France

Now you will learn how to keep the family car on the road in France! You need to know how to get petrol, oil, water and air for it and how to tackle a few minor problems which may arise.

j'apprends

Here are a few useful phrases which you need to become familiar with:

nettoyez le pare-brise

lavez la voiture

vérifiez l'eau

je voudrais de l'essence

vérifiez l'huile

vérifiez les pneus

You'll constantly be needing petrol, so let's see how to buy this.
Instead of the British system of stars, the French have only two types of petrol: *ordinaire* and *super*. *Ordinaire* is roughly 1 or 2 star, *super* is 3 or 4 star petrol.

Je voudrais	dix vingt trente	litres	d'ordinaire de super	s'il vous plaît.

Le plein	d'ordinaire de super de mélange de gas-oil	s'il vous plaît.

Answer to page 95 Quick quiz

1 *Parcotrain* long/short stay carparks.
2 Car-rental service
3 Radio taxis
4 SNCF bus service
5 *Métro* (underground)
6 High-speed métro
7 Bus stop
8 Airport link

Technical trouble

The most important phrase to remember is:

...... ne marche pas.

This means 'isn't working', and you can use it to say that any of these things aren't working on your car:

le clignotant droit (gauche)	the right (left) indicator
le phare droit (gauche)	the right (left) headlamp
le frein à main	the handbrake
l'essuie-glace	the windscreen wiper
le moteur	the motor
l'embrayage	the clutch

Other difficulties:

j'ai un pneu crevé	I have a flat tyre
je suis en panne d'essence	I've run out of petrol

A *j'écoute* You will now hear ten dialogues. Note down on your copy of the chart below what each customer wants. The first five involve buying petrol and having things checked or cleaned, while the second five are about cars which have developed problems.

	petrol	1st request	2nd request	3rd request
1				
2				
3				
4				
5				
6				
7				
8				
9				
10				

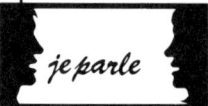

je parle Your partner is the garage attendant.

Ask for the following:

1 30 litres of super.
2 20 litres of 2 star.
3 Fill your car up with super.
4 Have the oil checked.
5 Have the windscreen wiped, the tyres checked and get the tank filled with 4 star.
6 Buy 40 litres of 2 star and get the car washed.
7 Get the water level checked and ask for 20 litres of 3 star.
8 Fill the tank up with ordinary petrol and get the oil checked.
9 Buy 20 litres of 3 star.
10 Buy 10 litres of super and have the tyre pressures checked.

Cette voiture est décapotable. C'est une voiture hors-série, une voiture spéciale, fabriquée par des enthousiastes.

Here are some more parts of a car which you might have trouble with or need to replace:

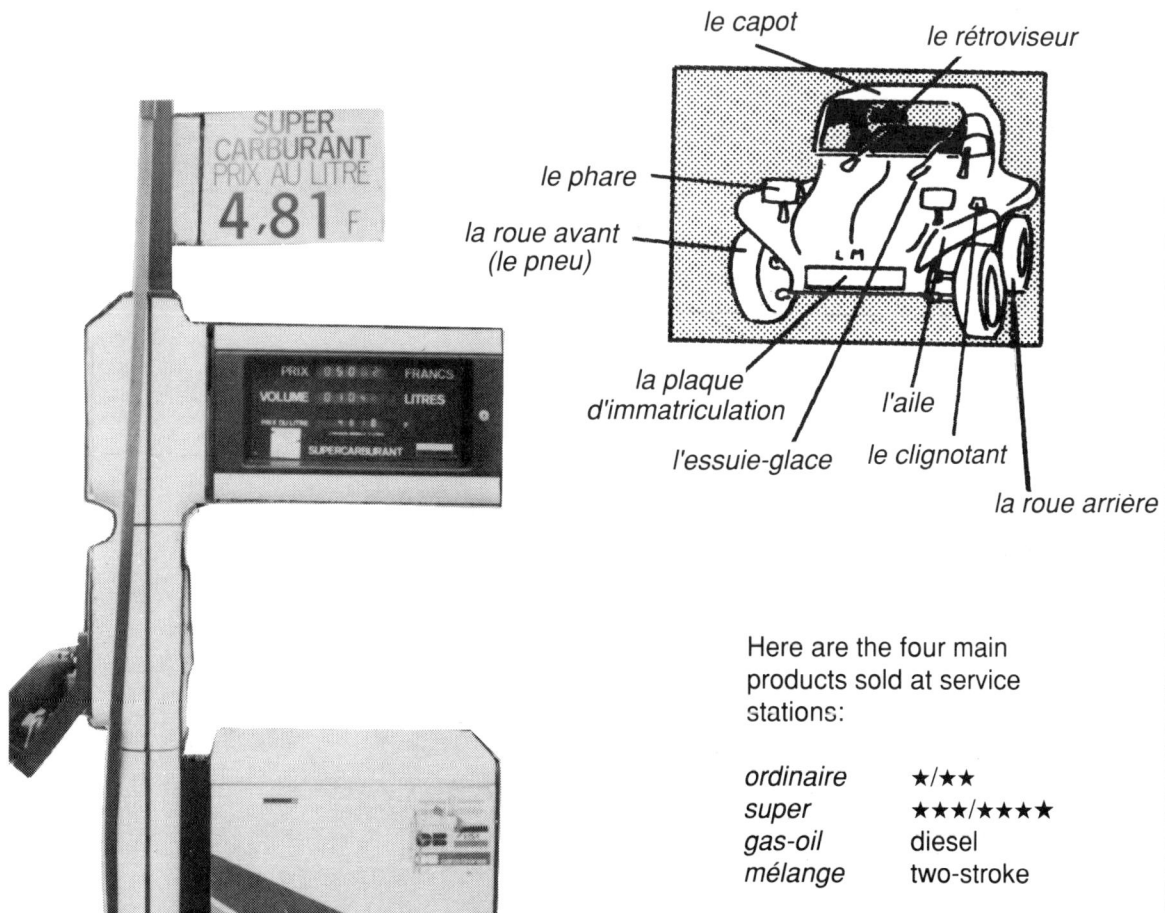

le capot

le rétroviseur

le phare

la roue avant (le pneu)

la plaque d'immatriculation

l'essuie-glace

l'aile

le clignotant

la roue arrière

SUPER CARBURANT PRIX AU LITRE **4,81** F

Here are the four main products sold at service stations:

ordinaire	★/★★
super	★★★/★★★★
gas-oil	diesel
mélange	two-stroke

Asking for parts

If your car breaks down, you will find yourself having to get hold of a particular spare part *(une pièce de rechange)*. The salesperson will ask what kind of car you have:

C'est pour quelle voiture?	What car is it for?
Vous avez quelle voiture?	What car have you got?

Remember that all cars are **une** words.

C'est pour une Ford.	It's for a Ford.
Nous avons une Ford.	We've got a Ford.

je parle

In French:

1 Ask for twenty litres of 2 star petrol.
2 Say the clutch on your car isn't working.
3 Ask for oil.
4 Say you've got a burst tyre.
5 Say you've run out of petrol.
6 Tell the garage that you've got a Metro.
7 Tell the garage man to wash the car.
8 Say you want your tyres checked.
9 Say the windscreen wiper isn't working.
10 Say you've got a Peugeot and the handbrake isn't working.

On roule sans permis!

Le garagiste répare une petite voiture un peu spéciale. Avec une voiture comme celle-ci on peut rouler sans permis de conduire!

celle-ci – this one	
rouler – drive	
le permis	
de conduire – driving licence	
sans – without	

In France it's now possible to drive a car even though you don't hold a current driving licence! The tiny car in this photograph is an example of the type of vehicle you can drive.

French drivers (with licences) hate these little cars: the top speed is 25mph and they think they're often driven by people who shouldn't be on the roads anyway!

Où es-tu allé?

To talk about where you went, you need to know these phrases:

je suis	allé	I went	
il est	venu	he came	
elle est	arrivé	she arrived	
on est	parti	we left	
tu es	entré	you entered	
vous êtes	sorti	you went out	

Using the examples in the block diagrams you can make sentences like the ones below.

Have a look at these and make sure you know what they mean.

1 *Il est allé à Paris.*
2 *Elle est partie à neuf heures.*
3 *On est arrivé à la gare.*
4 *Je suis allé au collège.*
5 *Il est entré dans la disco.*
6 *On est parti de l'école.*
7 *Il est parti avec Jill.*
8 *Je suis allé à Cardiff.*
9 *On est sorti ensemble.*
10 *Il est arrivé à Calais.*

11 *On est parti du cinéma.*
12 *Elle est arrivée.*
13 *On est allé au parc.*
14 *Il est entré dans la banque.*
15 *Il est sorti du cinéma.*
16 *Il est entré dans un café.*
17 *On est venu en autobus.*
18 *Elle est entrée en retard.*
19 *Il est allé à la piscine.*
20 *Je suis sorti avec Marie.*

Expressions utiles

avec	with
ensemble	together
en retard	late

These words will help you say **when** something happened:

dernier/dernière	last	l'été dernier	last summer
lundi dernier	last Monday	l'hiver dernier	last winter
la semaine dernière	last week	hier	yesterday
le mois dernier	last month	avant-hier	the day before yesterday
l'année dernière	last year	il y a quatre jours	four days ago

je lis

Here are some advertisements clipped from the newspaper *Le Figaro*.

How much of them can you understand?

Work in pairs. One of you should look at **this** page and the other at page 166.

Find out where your partner went on the days or during the periods shown and fill in a copy of the form below.

Note that you have to write down **where** she or he went, as well as **how** (by what means of transport) and **at what time** she or he arrived there.

Then, answer the questions your partner puts to you on the same subject. Make up the answers if you want to.

At the bottom of this page you'll see some phrases to help you with the **how** questions.

quand?	où?	par quel moyen de transport?	arrivée à…
hier soir			
lundi matin			
mardi soir			
mercredi après-midi			
jeudi soir			
vendredi matin			
samedi après-midi			
dimanche soir			
pendant les vacances de Pâques			
pendant les grandes vacances			

 en voiture

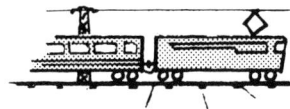 par le train

 en taxi

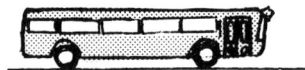 dans le car

 en bateau

 à pied

It's difficult to talk about pop music without mentioning names, yet those names go out of fashion so quickly it isn't worth saying who is popular in France at the time of writing. Pop music in France used to be a series of imitations of American and British styles. Nowadays, though, the French are producing songs which take advantage of modern electronic music technology but which sound very French.

The best way to find out about French popular music is to listen to some! In most parts of Britain it is possible to pick up one of these stations on long wave:

> *France Inter 164 kHz*
> *Europe Numéro Un 182 kHz*
> *RTL (Radio Télé Luxembourg) 236 kHz*

The first of these does not always play pop, and can be a bit middle-of-the-road, but the other two may give you a better idea of what young French people like to listen to.

Many young people in the Auvergne (central France), for example, do not listen to the major national stations, but to *RSDD (Radio Show Disque Danse)* a pop-only FM station.

On est fou de musique!

Les jeunes Françaises et Français sont tous aussi fous de musique que les jeunes dans les pays anglo-saxons. Ils achètent énormément de disques, de cassettes et de disques compacts.

> *fou/fous de* – mad about

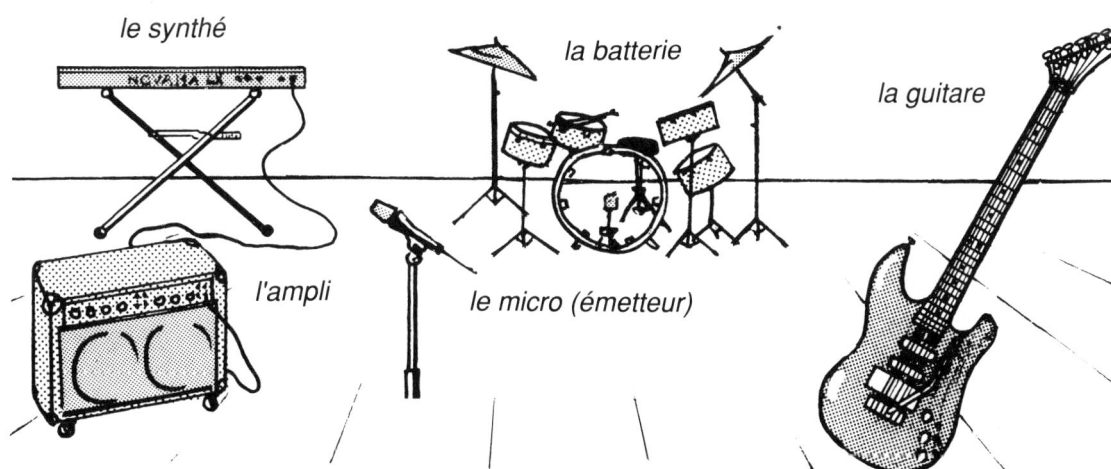

le synthé

la batterie

la guitare

l'ampli

le micro (émetteur)

En route!

ESSO Libre-service

SUPER
PRIX AU LITRE
4·71 F

Dialogue 1

Cliente	Bonjour, Monsieur.
Garagiste	Bonjour, Madame.
Cliente	Faites le plein, s'il vous plaît.
Garagiste	Oui, Madame – ordinaire ou super?
Cliente	Super, s'il vous plaît, et puis vérifiez l'huile, s'il vous plaît.
Garagiste	Bien, Madame.

Dialogue 2

Cliente	Bonjour, Monsieur.
Garagiste	Bonjour, Madame.
Cliente	J'ai des problèmes avec ma voiture.
Garagiste	Ah oui – qu'est-ce qui ne va pas?
Cliente	Le pare-brise est cassé…
Garagiste	Ah…
Cliente	Le clignotant gauche ne marche pas…
Garagiste	Oh…
Cliente	J'ai un pneu crevé…et puis je suis en panne d'essence.
Garagiste	Ah oui…alors effectivement…

Dialogue 3

Client	Bonjour, Madame.
Garagiste	Bonjour, Monsieur.
Client	J'ai un problème avec ma voiture – le phare gauche ne marche pas…
Garagiste	Et qu'est-ce que vous avez comme voiture, Monsieur?
Client	C'est une Ford…une Sierra.
Garagiste	Bien…

Dialogue 4

Client	Bonjour, Madame – je suis tombé en panne d'essence…ma voiture est à deux kilomètres d'ici sur la route nationale 41. Pouvez-vous m'aider, s'il vous plaît?
Garagiste	Oui, Monsieur…je peux vous prêter un bidon d'essence…
Client	Merci bien, Madame.

DIRECTIONS

VERS LA A 1

Mélange

STATION SERVICE

VOUS N'AVEZ PAS LA PRIORITÉ

SUPER CARBURANT

Feux à 100 mètres

Toutes directions

SERREZ À DROITE

FIN DE L'AUTOROUTE

Attention: voie bus

CÉDEZ LE PASSAGE

BOULEVARD PÉRIPHÉRIQUE

Parking à 300 mètres

PÉAGE À 800 MÈTRES

trois... deux... un...TOP!

j'écris

Once again, you have a second or two in which to find some way of answering the question! The family car has stopped at a service station because a few things are wrong with it and you need to buy petrol. You are talking to the forecourt attendant. Answer as fast as you can before the bleep!

1 Imagine that you are staying with your French penfriend. You are alone in the house when the phone rings. Write a note for your friend saying that Marie-Claire rang to invite you both to go to the cinema with her. Your friend should ring her back.

Remember that your French does not have to be perfect, but you must get the message across somehow.

2 Write the phrase used to sign off a formal letter, then check that you've got it right! If you've made a mistake, write it out again!

3 Your French friend sends you the following postcard.

Imagine that you are sending one back from your home town. Write it, but don't use too much of the material in the card below.

DOUCE LOIRE
Ein' grand' plat', su' l' canal, la grand'Nature, héreuse
D'y i' barcer lés song'ries du vieux pére, en béret,
Qui cass' la croût', tout seul, su' l'ieau, et on dirait
Ein' p'tit coin d'Paradis dans sa paix merveilleuse.

Une grande plate, sur le canal... La grande Nature, heureuse
D'y bercer les songeries du vieux père, en béret,
Qui casse la croûte, tout seul, sur l'eau, et on dirait
Un petit coin de Paradis dans sa paix merveilleuse.

Emile Joulain
L'gâs Mile

Doué-la-Fontaine
le 12 Août

Je suis à Doué-la-Fontaine depuis la semaine dernière. Il fait très chaud. Hier, on est allé voir les arènes. Elles ont été construites par les romains

A bientôt
Alain

Edition ALTO Résidence Santa Lina Bt B Route des Sanguinaires
20000 Ajaccio Tél: (95) 21.30.74. (Copyright by Alto)

M. COX
Eastern House
BLACMINSTER
EVESHAM
WORCESTERSHIRE
EV2 1NR

ANGLETERRE

DL 1009

les arènes – amphitheatres

4 Write a letter to the Hotel L'Europe in Cholet. You and your friend would like to stay for one night on the 1st August. Set this up, and ask about where you can park your car.

5   Write a letter in answer to the one on the right. Make sure that you answer all the questions in it.

Avignon, le 21 mai.

Cher Peter,

Dominique et Richard ont été enchantés de passer des vacances avec toi. Ils voudraient te revoir l'été prochain. Est-ce-que c'est possible en juillet ou en août ?

Dominique est actuellement en vacances en Alsace et Richard passe son permis de conduire la semaine prochaine.
Et toi ! Qu'est-ce que tu as fait depuis les dernières vacances ?
Et ta famille ! Comment va-t-elle ? Est ce que tes parents vont venir nous voir ? Je serais très contente de les connaître.

Bien amicalement

Madame Benoist

Have a look at this advertisement. Can you recognise all the features of the car? Here are a few words to help you:

la lunette – rear window
AR (arrière) – rear

les feux – lights
la vitre – pane (of glass)

You should be able to:

1 buy petrol for the family car;

2 have the tyres, water level and oil checked;

3 have the windscreen cleaned or the car washed;

4 tell a mechanic that something is wrong with your car;

5 say what kind of car you have;

6 talk about where you went at some time in the past.

je travaille

RÉPERTOIRE

La voiture

le pare-brise	windscreen
le pneu	tyre
le clignotant	indicator
le phare	headlight
le frein	brake
le frein à main	handbrake
l'essuie-glace	windscreen wiper
le moteur	motor
l'embrayage	clutch
le capot	roof
le rétroviseur	rear view mirror
la roue	wheel
l'aile	wing
l'essence	petrol
de l'eau	water
de l'huile	oil
de l'air	air
du mélange	two stroke mix

What services does this garage offer?

STATION SERVICE
TOTAL
Graissage Complet

GARAGE

ACCESSOIRES ★ PNEUS ★ BATTERIES

Révision Générale
MISE au POINT de
TOUS MOTEURS

Téléphone : 73 91 35 14
C. C. P. 1221-72 C
SIRET 304 695 307 (76 A 42)
R. M Clermont-Fd 5307

PIERRE ROBERT
24, avenue de Grande-Bretagne
63000 CLERMONT FERRAND

Station
d'Equilibrage

Le 26 DECEMBRE 1985
(Prière de rappeler cette date lors du règlement)

M. EDDEWARDS - TALBOT N° HKV32V - 30657 kms -

Doit

COUTY 63000

Remplacement des plaquettes de frein avant, dégripper les étriers, régler les freins arrière, essais :		
1 H 50 à 74,95	112,43	
1 jeu de plaquettes de frein		172,00
	112,43	172,00
T.V.A. 18,60 %	20,91	31,99
	133,34	203,99
		133,34
NET A PAYER		337,33

Getting money while in France

Now you will learn how to change money or travellers' cheques in a French bank.

CRÉDIT AGRICOLE

SOCIÉTÉ GÉNÉRALE

The first problem you may meet is actually finding a bank because banks don't always have the word *banque* displayed above them.

It's better to look for the word *crédit* or to know the names of the main banks: *Crédit Agricole, BNP (Banque Nationale de Paris), Société Générale, Crédit Lyonnais* and so forth.

You usually have the paperwork sorted out at the counter and get the money at the cash-desk *(la caisse)*. The bank clerk will say:

> *Passez à la caisse, s'il vous plaît.*   Go to the cash-desk, please

Frequently, you will see a sign *change* or *bureau de change*, in areas where tourists are common.

It is likely that you will have either cash *(de l'argent liquide)* or travellers' cheques. If you're changing sterling for francs, all you need is the money, but if you're changing travellers' cheques you will need your passport and perhaps your address in France (your hotel or campsite).

Sur cette photo on voit une banque qui s'appelle Crédit Industriel de l'Ouest (CIO). La banque est à Doué-la-Fontaine dans la vallée de la Loire.

on voit – you see

1 *Cette dame change environ cent livres en francs français.*

Elle est au comptoir, et non à la caisse. Le banquier examine les chèques de la dame et remplit un formulaire.

2 *Maintenant le banquier écrit la date sur un chèque.*

environ – about
une livre – a pound (**un** *livre* is the word for a book)
le comptoir – the counter
la caisse – the cash-desk
remplit – fills in

3   *Le banquier regarde le passeport de la dame.*

Il doit être certain que les chèques sont à elle. Ensuite, il lui dit: 'Passez à la caisse, madame'.

4   *Elle va à la caisse. Là, un autre banquier lui donne de l'argent français.*

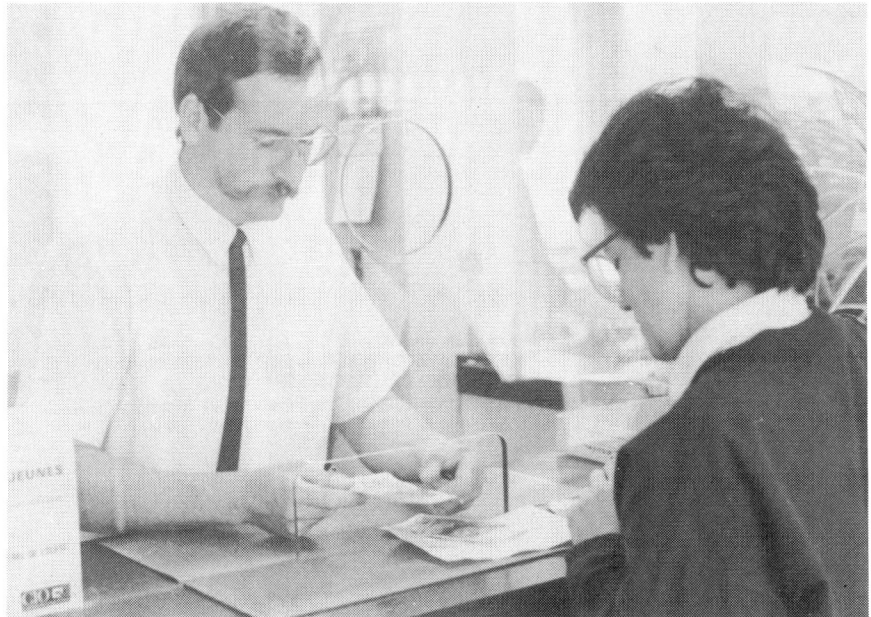

Expressions utiles

le chèque – the cheque
le passeport – the passport
la livre – the pound
le formulaire – the form
la caisse – the cash-desk

À la banque

Je voudrais changer	un chèque de voyage deux cheques de voyage		en francs s'il vous plaît.
	dix vingt trente	livres sterling	

j'écoute A

You will now hear ten people changing either cash or cheques into francs. Listen out for whether they are giving the bank cash or cheques, for the amount they are changing and for any other question asked and answered, such as *Quel est le taux de change?* (What is the rate of exchange?). Fill in your answers on your copy of the chart below.

	cash or cheques?	amount?	other question?
1			
2			
3			
4			
5			
6			
7			
8			
9			
10			

je travaille

Can you pair up each currency with the country it comes from?

lire	Schilling	l'Autriche	l'Afrique du Sud
cruzeiro	franc	le Japon	la Chine
rouble	dinar	la France	le Finlande
dollar	Krona	l'Espagne	l'Allemagne
peseta	yen	la Yougoslavle	l'Italie
zloty	yuan	l'URSS	les États-Unis
Mark	Rand	la Pologne	le Brésil

Vous faites le change?

Dialogue 1

Employé de banque	Bonjour, Mademoiselle.
Susan	Bonjour, Monsieur. Je voudrais changer des chèques de voyage, s'il vous plaît.
Employé de banque	Oui. Vous avez votre passeport?
Susan	Oui…voilà.
Employé de banque	Merci…très bien. Vous voulez changer combien?
Susan	Je voudrais changer trente livres sterling en francs.
Employé de banque	Très bien. Signez ici, s'il vous plaît. Bien. Vous avez une adresse en France?
Susan	Oui, je suis à l'hôtel Europa, avenue de la Gare.
Employé de banque	Bien…passez à la caisse, s'il vous plaît.

Dialogue 2

Employé de banque	Bonjour, jeune homme.
Peter	Bonjour Monsieur, je voudrais changer trente livres sterling en francs français, s'il vous plaît.
Employé de banque	Oui…il y a une commission de deux pour cent…
Peter	D'accord…
Employé de banque	Bien…passez à la caisse, s'il vous plaît.

Dialogue 3

Mary	Bonjour, Monsieur…je voudrais changer trente livres sterling en francs, s'il vous plaît. Quel est le taux de change?
Employé de banque	La livre est à dix francs trente, Mademoiselle…
Mary	Vous acceptez les Eurochèques, Monsieur?
Employé de banque	Oui, Mademoiselle.

Dialogue 4

Monsieur	Bonjour Madame, je voudrais acheter des livres sterling.
Employé de banque	Oui Monsieur…combien en voulez-vous?
Monsieur	J'en voudrais pour 500 francs.

Saying how something is being done

Here are a few words (adverbs) which will help you:

vite	quickly	*fort*	loudly
lentement	slowly	*trop*	too much
bien	well	*beaucoup*	a lot
mal	badly	*un peu*	a little
doucement	quietly	*pas beaucoup*	not much
bruyamment	noisily	*souvent*	often
pas souvent	not often		

See if you can understand what's being said here:

1 *Il mange bruyamment.*
2 *Elle travaille bien.*
3 *Marie mange vite.*
4 *Tu chantes fort.*
5 *Elle marche lentement.*
6 *Elle joue bien au tennis.*
7 *La voiture va vite.*
8 *Il parle vite.*
9 *Il regarde souvent la télé.*
10 *Jean parle trop souvent.*

je parle

In French, say something about:

1 the speed of a Ferrari.
2 the way George is eating.
3 how well you sing.
4 the way someone in the class is working.
5 the speed of the school bus *(le car scolaire)*.
6 the way you speak French.
7 how often you go dancing.
8 how well you play tennis.
9 a sport you play well.
10 how often you watch TV.

je travaille

1 Your teacher will tell you roughly what the rate of exchange is, that is, how many francs you can get for a pound. When you know what it is, look at the pictures on pages 44, 47, and 53 and decide how much the various things shown would cost in pounds and pence.

2 Using the current rate of exchange, write the following amounts in both francs and sterling (pounds and pence) into your exercise book. When you go to France, you will find it useful to have learned these amounts:

50	centimes	....
1	franc	....
5	francs	....
10	francs	....
20	francs	....
50	francs	....
100	francs	....

Comparing things and people

When you want to compare two things or people, you'll need a **describing word** (adjective) *(petit, intelligent etc.)* and the word *plus*, which means **more**, or *moins*, which means **less**.

Have a look at these sentences:

*Pierre est **plus grand** que Georges.*

*Georges est **plus petit** que Pierre.*

*Marie est **plus intelligente** que Claire.*

*Claire est **moins intelligente** que Marie.*

je travaille Draw small sketches in your exercise book to show you understand these comparisons.

1 *Marie est plus intelligente que Georges.*
2 *Henri est moins grand que Marie.*
3 *La gare est plus jolie que le supermarché.*
4 *Le supermarché est moins grand que l'épicerie.*
5 *Le stylo est plus cher que le crayon.*
6 *La cassette est moins longue que le disque.*
7 *La cathédrale est moins longue que la gare.*
8 *Le garçon est moins grand que la fille.*
9 *La voiture est plus rapide que le vélo.*
10 *Le vélomoteur est plus cher que le vélo.*

If two things or people are about the same in some way, there is a special way of saying this. The phrase you need is:

> *...aussi...que...*   (...as...as...)

and when it is used it looks like this:

*George est **aussi** intelligent **que** Pierre.*

je parle Look around you in the classroom. With your partner, compare the people you see with one another!

Work in pairs. One of you should look at **this** page and the other at page 167.

Both you and your partner are looking at the six drawings below. The only difference is that the positions of the six drawings are different.

Your job is to try to be the first to work out where your partner's drawings are placed.

Take turns to ask each other questions about the drawings. You need to ask, for example, about your partner's picture three *(image numéro trois): Est-ce que le nez du monsieur est plus long que le nez de la dame?* Then continue to ask questions until you discover which of your pictures is like your partner's picture three.

1

2

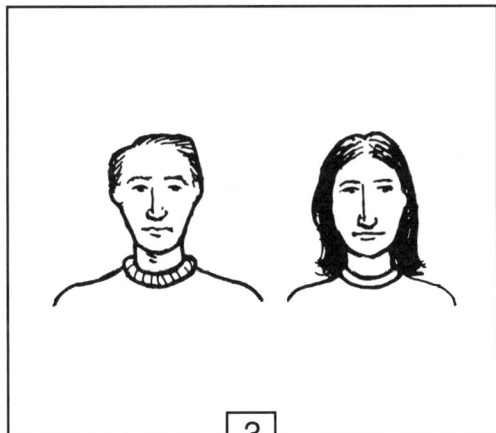

3

4

5

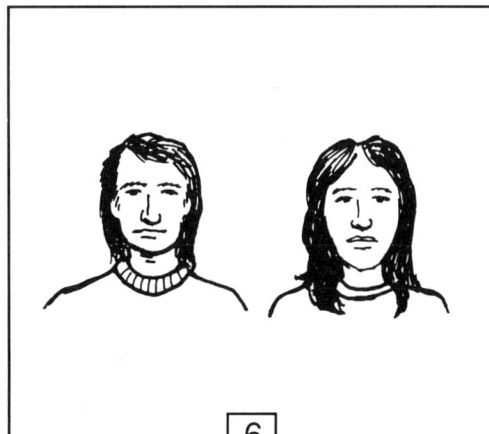

6

De l'argent français

There are four main banknotes in use in France (you won't see the others unless inflation gets much worse or you get rich!):

un billet de 20 francs

un billet de 50 francs

un billet de 100 francs

un billet de 200 francs (shown in the photograph below)

Your teacher will tell you how much they are worth at the moment.

You must get used to working out how much these are worth. For example, if the rate of exchange were 10F 50 to the pound, the notes would be worth roughly:

20F	£1.90
50F	£4.76
100F	£9.52
200F	£19.05

13F *le kilo*   **25F**   **10F** *pièce*   **895F**   **65F**

Use the rate given here or find it in the newspaper and work out how much the articles with these price tags are worth in British money:

DISTRIBUTEUR DE BILLETS

CHEQUES POSTAUX

Voici une banque qui est toujours ouverte! C'est un distributeur automatique de billets.

Bientôt, les étrangers vont utiliser les machines françaises.

DIRECTIONS

CAISSE

CET APPAREIL NE REND PAS LA MONNAIE

COURS DES MONNAIES ÉTRANGÈRES

ACHAT

Bureau de change

VENTE

CHANGE

INTRODUISEZ UNE PIÈCE DE 10F DANS LA FENTE

CAISSE ÉCLAIR

APPAREIL HORS SERVICE

trois... C
deux...
un...*TOP!*

Once again, you have a second or two in which to find some way of answering the question! You are in a bank, changing some travellers' cheques. Answer as fast as you can before the bleep!

j'écris

1 Your French friend sends you a postcard. Later, when you go on holiday, you write one too, but you are not enjoying your holiday. Write the card, but don't use too much of the material in the card below.

> Saint Malo
> le 5 juin
> Je suis bien arrivée à Saint Malo. Il fait un temps splendide. J'aime beaucoup la Bretagne. Le soir, on mange souvent des crêpes. Demain, je vais visiter le fort. Je passe de très bonnes vacances.
> Meilleurs souvenirs
> Christine
>
> A BADGER
> Little Ravelin
> Ravelin Gardens
> NORTHAMPTON
> NN3 4 JL
> ANGLETERRE
>
> 3.15.78.0011   49.125

2 Imagine that you are staying with your French penfriend, but that you have to go out soon. You are alone in the house when a French girl called Magali phones. Write a note for your friend saying that she phoned, and that she left her bag here when she visited your friend yesterday. She wants to know if she can come and pick it up this evening.

Remember that your French does not have to be perfect, but you must get the message across somehow.

3 Write a letter to the youth hostel in Lapalisse. You and your friend would like to stay there for three nights from the 3rd to the 6th August.

You should be able to:

1 find a bank;

2 ask an official to change your money or travellers' cheques for you;

3 understand her or his questions to you;

4 find out the exchange rate for the day;

5 say how something is being done;

6 compare things and people.

RÉPERTOIRE

À la banque

la caisse	cash-desk
change ⎫	
bureau de change ⎬	bank
un chèque de voyage	travellers' cheque
une livre	a pound
un livre	a book
un banquier	a bank official
un formulaire	a form
un comptoir	a counter
un passeport	a passport
le sterling	sterling (British money)

j'écris

You and your family are driving to your French friend's home when your car develops a fault, and you have to stop for repairs.

The family are not English speakers, and they are not on the telephone so you decide to send a telegram. It is still usual to send these in France.

Your job is to write the telegram! You can use your exercise book. Bear in mind that you have to pay for every word... yet the family are going to have to understand that you're going to arrive several hours late!

How to talk to the doctor or dentist

The first thing to know about health care in France is that it has to be paid for on the spot, even if you are able to claim a refund later. All doctors and dentists in France have a cash drawer in their desks! A chat to a doctor could set you back 75 francs. So it is important that, before you leave England, someone in your family obtains a form E111 from your local office of the DHSS.

This allows you to be cared for by the French health service, which means that you can claim from them a sizeable proportion of any money you spend on doctors, dentists or medicines. (You may also decide to take out a separate travel insurance policy to be doubly sure.)

You must keep the *feuille de soins* (a form on which the doctor or dentist says what treatment you have been given) and stick onto it the *vignettes* (labels) which you will find on any medicines which the doctor or dentist prescribes for you.

une feuille de soins

une vignette

Expressions utiles

je ne me sens pas bien	I don't feel well
je me sens malade	I feel ill
j'ai de la température / *j'ai de la fièvre*	I have a temperature
j'ai mal à l'estomac	I have a stomach-ache
j'ai mal aux reins	I have back-ache
je me suis foulé la cheville	I've sprained my ankle
je me suis égratigné le genou	I've grazed my knee
je me suis coupé le doigt	I've cut my finger
j'ai le nez bouché	My nose is blocked
j'ai mal à la gorge	I have a sore throat
j'ai des nausées	I feel sick
j'ai envie de vomir	I think I'm going to be sick
j'ai des boutons	I've got spots
j'ai des douleurs	I've got pains
j'ai un coup de soleil	I've got sunburn

Let's begin by looking at the way you say that you have a pain in some part of your body. These expressions use the **link words** which you met on page 60.

which you met on page 60.

j'apprends

J'ai mal...

à la tête

au cou
à l'épaule
à la poitrine

au bras

à la main

au genou

au pied

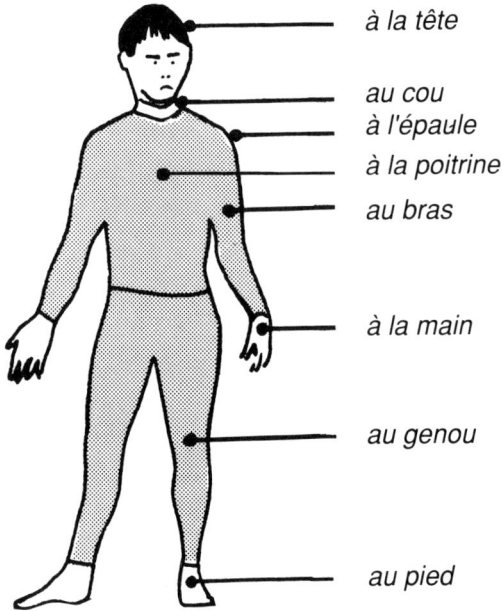

37° is the normal body temperature. If it is more you should be telling a doctor:

J'ai de la température.

If it's very high:

J'ai beaucoup de fièvre.

To say what your temperature is, say 38.5, just say the numbers:

J'ai trente-huit cinq.

A

j'écoute

You'll now hear a series of ten patients telling their doctors their troubles. On your copy of the chart below, write the symptoms they describe.

There may be up to four for each patient.

	symptom 1	symptom 2	symptom 3	symptom 4
1				
2				
3				
4				
5				
6				
7				
8				
9				
10				

Work in pairs. One of you should look at **this** page and the other at page 168.

In this game, you and your partner will take it in turns to play the parts of patient and doctor. For the first three interviews you play the part of the patient, and your partner is the doctor.

For each interview, choose one of the sets of symptoms below and answer your partner's questions in line with them.

	symptômes	depuis...
1	mal à la gorge mal à la tête fièvre	2–3 jours
2	température élevée boutons les yeux qui pleurent	1 jour
3	fièvreux mal de poitrine nausées	2–3 jours

For the second set of three interviews, you are the doctor and your partner is the patient. Here are some technical details to help you make up your diagnosis in each case.

Make your diagnosis and prescribe whatever is necessary.

Your teacher will check your diagnosis to see how you have coped!

	symptômes	depuis...	diagnostique	remède
a	mal au foie	1 jour	jaunisse	antibiotique une semaine au lit régime spécial
b	mal à la gorge mal à la tête fièvre	2–3 jours	angine (tonsilitis)	antibiotique 3 jours au lit
c	nez bouché éternuement mal à la gorge	4 jours	rhume (cold)	sirop gouttes pour le nez (drops)
d	mal au bas ventre sur le côté – douleur intense mal au coeur	une demie-heure	appendicite	à l'hôpital – vite
e	température élevée boutons (spots)	1 jour	rougeole (measles)	antibiotiques éviter la lumière rester au lit

Expressions utiles

j'ai des nausées	I feel sick
j'ai les yeux qui pleurent	my eyes are running
des douleurs fortes	strong pains
mal au foie	pain in liver
des brûlures de gorge	sore throat
des boutons	spots
je vais vous faire une ordonnance	I'm going to write you a prescription
vous devez aller...	you must go
rester au lit	stay in bed
éviter la lumière	avoid the light
prenez ces pilules	take these tablets
du sirop	medicine
le bas ventre	lower abdomen

Here are a few problems which you might have to deal with while on holiday
in France if you are really unlucky:

J'ai été piqué par une guêpe/abeille/un moustique/taon.
I've been stung/bitten by a wasp/bee/mosquito/horse fly

Un serpent m'a mordu.
A snake has bitten me.

J'ai mangé un champignon vénéneux.
I've eaten a poisonous mushroom.

Chez le dentiste

*Robert est chez le dentiste. Le dentiste examine les dents
de Robert. Robert a un problème: il a une dent cariée.
Le dentiste va utiliser sa roulette pour enlever ce qui est
mauvais, puis il va plomber la dent.*

une dent – a tooth
la roulette – drill
ce qui est – that which is
plomber – fill
cariée – decayed

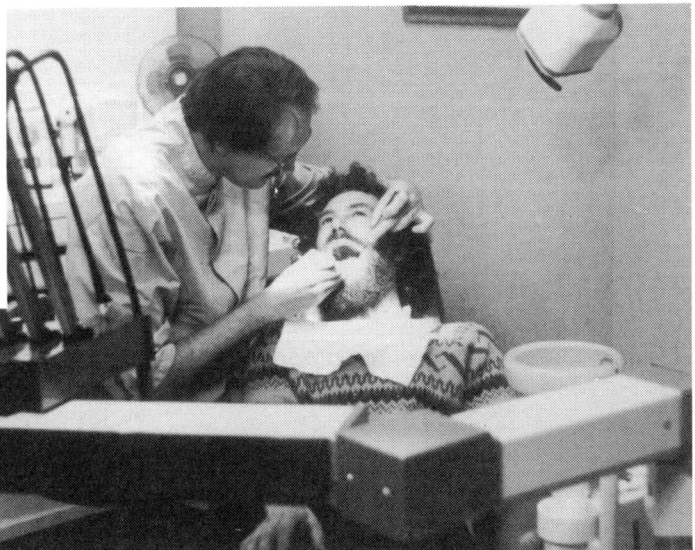

DOCTEUR J.P. CREPELLIERE
CHIRURGIEN-DENTISTE

une dent

B
j'écoute

You will now hear ten patients in a doctor's or dentist's surgery.
See if you can decide in each case what treatment they are going to
receive. Fill in your answers on your copy of the chart below.

	treatment
1	
2	
3	
4	
5	
6	
7	
8	
9	
10	

In France, people tend to use their livers as scapegoats for anything that goes wrong
with their health.

You will also notice that an English person will probably say 'Ow' if she or he is in pain.
In France, they say *'Aïe!'*

Here are some expressions which the French use a lot, and which look very strange to
us. It's not always altogether clear what they mean by them!

J'ai mal au foie.	I have a pain in the liver.
Elle a une crise de foie.	She is having a liver crisis.
Georges a le foie sensible.	George has a sensitive liver.

Saying something happened to you, or to someone else

Imagine you've just been to the doctor's and you're telling your French friend what happened there.

Here is some help in doing this:

me (m')   me/to me
lui   to him/to her

je travaille

See if you can understand these sentences:

1 *Il m'a fait une piqûre.*
2 *Elle m'a donné des cachets.*
3 *Il lui a donné du sirop.*
4 *Elle m'a dit: 'Reste au lit!'*
5 *Il lui a donné une ordonnance.*
6 *Elle m'a donné des cachets.*
7 *Il lui a donné de l'aspirine.*
8 *Elle lui a parlé.*
9 *Il m'a donné une bouteille de sirop.*
10 *Elle lui a fait une piqûre.*

Expressions utiles

prends   take
une ordonnance   a prescription
reste   stay

je lis

Voici une ambulance. L'étoile bleue est l'insigne typique d'une ambulance. Les ambulances sont souvent payantes – des compagnies privées organisent le service.

une étoile – star
l'insigne – sign
souvent – often
payant – paying, have to be paid for

This is the instruction sheet from an antibiotic prescribed for a mouth infection by a dentist. Imagine that you were given this to take!

Try to discover:

1 what side effects it could have;

2 when you should **not** use it;

3 what the adult dose is;

4 with what you may take it;

5 when you should take it.

ProAmpi

PIVAMPICILLINE BASE

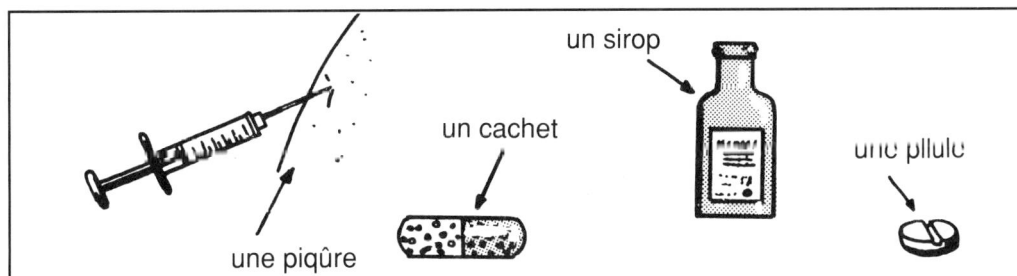

Antibiotique à large spectre

Indications thérapeutiques :
infections à germes Gram + et − sensibles,
infections odontostomatologiques, O.R.L.,
urinaires, couverture antibiotique.

Effets indésirables :
Manifestations allergiques : prurit, urticaire, rashs cutanés, œdème de Quincke.
Troubles digestifs : nausées, vomissements, diarrhées, candidose.

Mise en garde :
Toute manifestation allergique doit être signalée au médecin.

Contre-indications :
Allergie aux pénicillines.
Traitement par l'allopurinol.

Précautions d'emploi :
Prévenir le médecin traitant en cas de :
– insuffisance rénale,
– antécédents allergiques,
– manifestations cutanées d'origine allergique,
– prise concomitante d'autres médicaments.

Posologie :
Adultes et enfants de plus de 12 ans :
● Posologie usuelle : 1 g/jour, en 2 ou 3 prises.
● Dans les infections plus sévères et / ou chroniques, augmenter les doses jusqu'à 2 à 3 g par jour.
Dans tous les cas se conformer à la prescription médicale.

Mode d'emploi :
Avaler les comprimés sans les sucer ni les croquer, au cours des repas ou avec un verre d'eau non gazeuse ou du lait.

Composition - Présentation :
Pivampicilline base (DCI) .... 350 mg
Excipient : Carboxyméthylamidon. Amidon. Methylcellulose 15 cps
Magnésium (stéarate de) .... q.s.p. un comprimé

Boîte de 16 comprimés sous emballage alvéolaire, soit 5,6 g de Pivampicilline par étui.

A.M.M., n° 319.154.9

TABLEAU A   REMBOURSÉ PAR LA SÉCURITÉ SOCIALE 70 %

Laboratoires PHARMEUROP
Division Pharmaceutique de F.S.P.
8, IMPASSE DE LA MONTJOIE - 93210 LA PLAINE SAINT DENIS

---

16 COMPRIMÉS

ProAmpi

PIVAMPICILLINE BASE

---

un sirop

un cachet

une pilule

une piqûre

Sur cette page vous voyez quelques journaux français.

Il y a des journaux nationaux et des journaux régionaux.

Les journaux régionaux sont bien plus importants en France qu'en Angleterre.

'Le Matin', 'Libération', 'Le Monde', 'France Soir' et 'La Tribune de l'Economie' s'achètent partout en France; 'Le dauphiné libéré' est un journal local.

'Le 74' est un journal gratuit.

voyez – see
quelques – a few
s'achètent – can be bought
partout – everywhere
gratuit – free of charge

As in this country, French newspapers tend to support various political parties. '*Le Monde*' is liberal or slightly left of centre; you might compare it to our 'Independent' or 'Guardian'. '*Le Figaro*' and '*L'Aurore*' are conservative newspapers (a little like our 'Daily Telegraph' and 'TheTimes') whilst '*L'Humanité*' is a communist paper like the 'Morning Star', but with a much larger circulation. '*France-Soir*' is just one example of several newpapers which are similar to our 'Daily Star' or 'Sun'.

Regional newspapers tend to avoid showing any strong political tendencies. The paper with the largest circulation is a regional paper '*Ouest-France*'.

J'ai mal!

Dialogue 1

Docteur	Bonjour, jeune homme. Qu'est-ce qui vous amène?
Martin	J'ai un mal de tête atroce, Docteur.
Docteur	Depuis quand avez-vous ça?
Martin	Depuis hier.
Docteur	Est-ce que vous avez mal à la gorge?
Martin	Oui, un peu.
Docteur	Ouvrez la bouche, s'il vous plaît. Ah oui. C'est bien rouge. Vous avez mal au dos?
Martin	Aussi, oui.
Docteur	Eh bien, vous avez la grippe…je vais vous faire une ordonnance.

Dialogue 2

Lisa	Bonjour, Monsieur.
Dentiste	Bonjour, Mademoiselle. Qu'est-ce qui vous amène?
Lisa	J'ai une dent qui me fait très mal.
Dentiste	Ah oui? Ouvrez la bouche, s'il vous plaît.
Lisa	Aïe!
Dentiste	Eh oui…vous avez une dent qui est mauvaise…je vais vous faire un plombage.

Dialogue 3

Derek	Bonjour, Monsieur.
Docteur	Bonjour, jeune homme. Qu'est-ce qui vous amène?
Derek	J'ai mal au coeur…et puis je pense que j'ai de la température.
Docteur	Hmm…depuis quand avez-vous cela?
Derek	Depuis avant-hier.
Docteur	Qu'est-ce que vous avez mangé avant-hier?
Derek	J'ai fait un grand repas avec des fruits de mer, Monsieur.
Docteur	Hmm…vous allez prendre deux de ces cachets tout de suite, et puis encore un cachet toutes les trois heures. Et puis je vais vous faire une ordonnance.

DIRECTIONS

CHIRURGIE **BUREAU D'ACCUEIL** **consultation**

SALLE D'ATTENTE PHARMACIE **Horaires des consultations**

MÉDECINE GÉNÉRALE

Clinique **Cabinet médical** ACCÈS RÉSERVÉ AU PERSONNEL

HÔPITAL

trois... deux... un...TOP! D

Once again, you have a second or two in which to find some way of reacting to what is said to you. Answer as quickly as you can before the bleep!

j'écris

1 Think back to your last holiday, then use the postcard below to help you write a card to an imaginary French penfriend. Try not to use too much of the material in the card below.

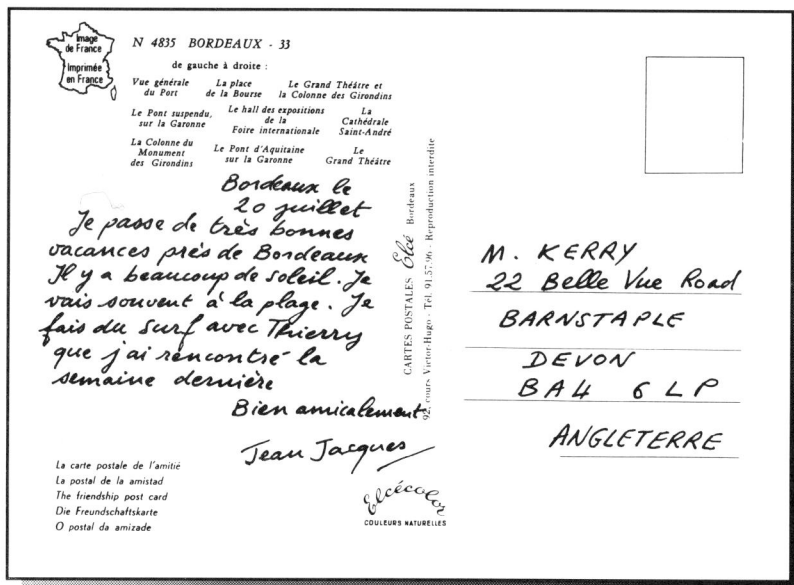

N 4835 BORDEAUX - 33

de gauche à droite :

Vue générale du Port *La place de la Bourse* *Le Grand Théâtre et la Colonne des Girondins*

Le Pont suspendu, sur la Garonne *Le hall des expositions de la Foire internationale* *La Cathédrale Saint-André*

La Colonne du Monument des Girondins *Le Pont d'Aquitaine sur la Garonne* *Le Grand Théâtre*

CARTES POSTALES *Elcé* Bordeaux
92 cours Victor-Hugo - Tél. 91.57.96 - Reproduction interdite

Bordeaux le 20 juillet
Je passe de très bonnes vacances près de Bordeaux. Il y a beaucoup de soleil. Je vais souvent à la plage. Je fais du surf avec Thierry que j'ai rencontré la semaine dernière.
Bien amicalement.
Jean Jacques

La carte postale de l'amitié
La postal de la amistad
The friendship post card
Die Freundschaftskarte
O postal da amizade

elcécolor
COULEURS NATURELLES

M. KERRY
22 Belle Vue Road
BARNSTAPLE
DEVON
BA4 6LP
ANGLETERRE

2 Write out the phrase used to sign off a formal letter, then check that you've got it right! If you've made a mistake, write it out again!

3 Write a letter to the Hôtel de Paris in Nîmes. You and your family would like to stay there for two nights during August. Find out whether you can have an evening meal in the hotel.

While in Paris your father lost his wallet. He has just received this letter, and has asked you to tell him what it's about. Do what you can! If you manage to get any idea at all of what this is about you'll be doing well!

Bureau des objets trouvés

25, rue de la Croix-Nivert, 75015 PARIS

Monsieur,

Un chauffeur de taxi nous a remis un porte-feuille dans lequel nous avons trouvé un permis de conduire à votre nom. Je suis en mesure de vous l'envoyer à votre adresse en Grande-Bretagne, mais je vous serais reconnaissant de bien vouloir me faire parvenir la somme de 25 francs à titre de remboursement des frais postaux.

je vous prie d'agréer, Monsieur, l'assurance de ma considération distinguée,

Pour le Secrétaire Général du Bureau des Objets Trouvés

Edmond Meunier

You should be able to:

1 describe simple health problems to a doctor or dentist;

2 understand the questions put to you by a doctor or dentist;

3 understand a doctor's or dentist's simpler advice or recommendations;

4 say what happened to you while you were at the doctor's or dentist's.

je cherche

How much of this prescription can you manage to decipher?!

RÉPERTOIRE

Chez le médecin

une feuille de soins	statement of treatment
une vignette	label
une température	temperature
la tête	the head
le cou	neck
l'épaule	shoulder
le bras	arm
la main	hand
le genou	knee
le pied	foot
une piqûre	sting, injection

Chez le dentiste

une dent	tooth
la roulette	drill
un plombage	filling
plomber	to fill
utiliser	to use

Divers

une guêpe	wasp
une abeille	bee
un moustique	mosquito
un serpent	snake
un champignon	mushroom/toadstool
un taon	horse fly

FRANÇOIS LALLEMAND

DOCTEUR EN MÉDECINE
DIPLÔMÉ DE STOMATOLOGIE
ANCIEN INTERNE DE L'HÔPITAL DE DREUX

25, RUE LUCAS - 03200 VICHY

TÉL : (70) 98-17-14

PHARMACIE DES SOURCES
P. JABOT
Docteur en Pharmacie
14 Avenue Aristide Briand
03200 VICHY

Buying things in the market

je lis

Voici un marché.
Les rues de cette petite ville sont remplies de caravanes et de camionnettes.

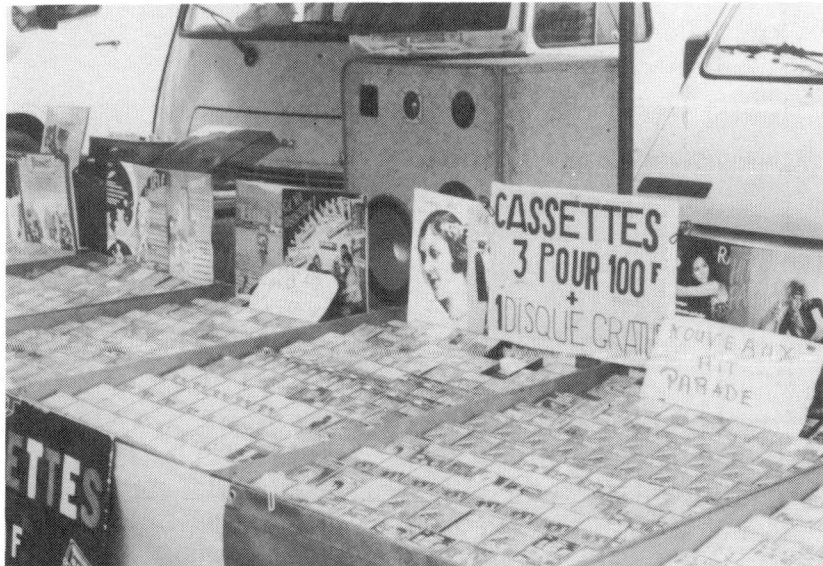

Dans un marché, il y a toutes sortes de choses. Voici, par exemple, des cassettes.
Trois cassettes pour 100 francs – c'est cher?

Expressions utiles

C'est combien, ça?	How much is that?
Vous en avez des moins chers?	Have you any that are cheaper?
C'est un peu cher, ça.	That's a bit expensive.

Est-ce que vous en avez en…?
Have you any in…?

In the space you put the colour, size, material, etc.

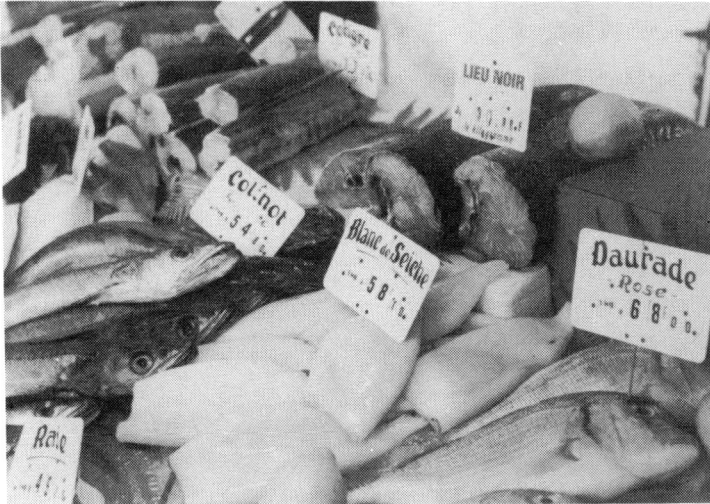

Dans ce marché il y a beaucoup de poissons.
Aimez-vous la poulpe sur la photo de droite?
Elle est mignonne, non?
Est-ce que c'est cher, la poulpe?

colinot – codling	congre – conger
raie – ray (skate)	lieu – pollack
daurade – gilt-head	poulpe – octopus

Depuis

This word is very handy for saying **how long** you've been doing something.

To use *depuis* properly you'll also need some **time** words:

un an	a year	une semaine	a week
un mois	a month	trois jours	3 days
une heure	an hour	5 minutes	5 minutes

je travaille

Have a go at making out what these sentences say:

1 J'apprends l'anglais depuis deux ans.
2 Je fais du judo depuis cinq ans.
3 Je regarde la télé depuis une heure.
4 Je parle avec Sylvie depuis 5 minutes.
5 Je lis le journal depuis une demi-heure.
6 Je joue au rugby depuis deux ans.
7 Je chante à l'église depuis trois mois.
8 J'apprends le français depuis quatre ans.
9 Je sors avec Linda depuis une semaine.
10 J'attends le train depuis dix minutes.

Expressions utiles

j'apprends	I learn	l'église	church
je fais	I do	je sors	I go out
je lis	I read	j'attends	I wait for
une demie	half	une demi-heure	half an hour

je lis

Cette dame vend
des sous-vêtements;
des slips et des
maillots de corps.

Est-ce que les
vêtements sont
chers?

C'est un grand
marché. On y vend
de tout. La ville est
envahie par le
marché tous les
quinze jours.

envahie – invaded
y – there
tous les – every
de tout – all kinds
          of things

Il y a des
étalages partout
dans le centre,
des deux côtés
de la rue.

étalages – stalls
partout – everywhere
côtés – sides

What size do you take?

Here are some possible questions and replies:

Quelle taille faites-vous?

Je fais du 36.

Vous chaussez du combien?

Vous faites quelle pointure?

Je fais du 36.

Qui/que

Both words mean **who**, **whom** or **which** in English. The problem is using the right one.

It helps if you know how to use **who** and **whom** in English.

1 *qui* means **who** or **which** when it means **the person or thing doing something:**

L'homme **qui** fume est grand.	The man, who is smoking, is tall.
La femme **qui** regarde la télé est malade.	The woman, who is watching TV, is ill.
Le professeur **qui** parle est content.	The teacher, who is talking, is happy.
Le chat **qui** miaule est noir.	The cat, which is miaowing, is black.
La dame **qui** travaille est jolie.	The lady, who is working, is pretty.

2 *que* or qu' mean **whom** or **which** when it means **the person or thing having something done to them:**

L'homme **que** j'ai rencontré est grand.	The man, whom I met, is tall.
La femme **que** j'ai vue était en retard.	The woman, whom I saw, was late.
Le professeur **qu'** il a cherché était au café.	The teacher, for whom he looked, was in the café.
Le chat **qu'** elle a trouvé est noir.	The cat, which she found, is black.
La dame **qu'** on aime bien n'est pas ici.	The lady, whom we like, isn't here.

If you find this hard don't worry – it is!

je travaille

Try guessing which word *qui* or *que* is need in these:

The English meanings appear below.

1 *La voiture......j'ai achetée est bleue.*
2 *Le garçon ......parle français est ici.*
3 *La fille......s'appelle Sharon est grande.*
4 *Le stylo......j'ai perdu est rouge.*
5 *Le chien......Marie a trouvé s'appelle Rover.*
6 *Le disque......est sur la table est cassé.*
7 *La montre......est rouge est la montre de Paul.*
8 *Le livre......j'ai acheté est de Charles Dickens.*
9 *La cassette......est dans mon sac est des '5 Stars'.*
10 *Le garçon......parle allemand est mon frère.*

1 The car, which I've bought, is blue.
2 The boy, who speaks French, is here.
3 The girl, who is called Sharon, is tall.
4 The pen, which I lost, is red.
5 The dog, which Marie found, is called Rover.
6 The record, which is on the table, is broken.
7 The watch, which is red, is Paul's watch.
8 The book, which I bought, is by Charles Dickens.
9 The cassette, which is in my bag, is by the '5 Stars'.
10 The boy, who is speaking German, is my brother.

je lis

Ce monsieur vend des téléphones.

La dame à gauche va échanger son vieux téléphone contre un téléphone très moderne.

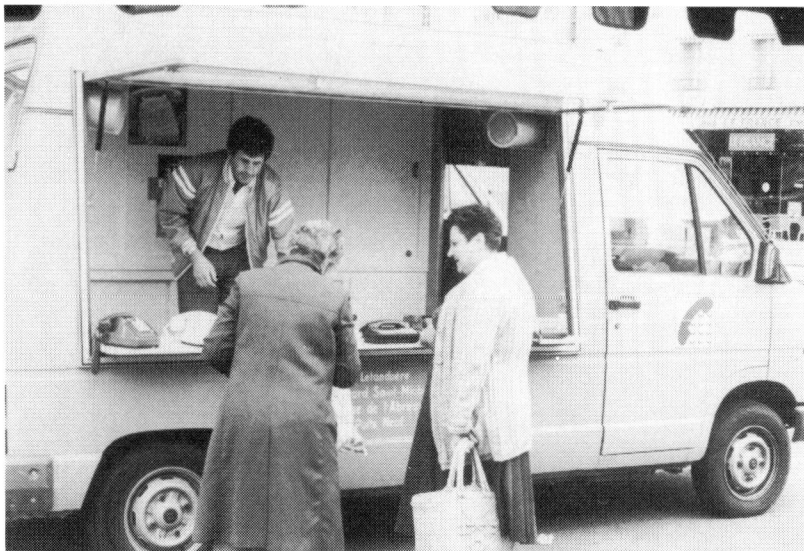

Cette dame vend des poules, des canards et des lapins au marché.

Souvent on vend des lapins angoras au marché: ce sont de gros lapins avec beaucoup de poils.

gros – big
poils – hair/fur

ce/cette/ces

Look at these useful words:

ce   this/that (for an **un** word *ce garçon* this boy)
cette   this/that (for an **une** word *cette fille* this girl)
ces   these/those

Have a look at these sentences. Do you understand them?

1 *J'aime bien **cette** émission.*
2 *Je préfère **ce** chocolat.*
3 *Il aime **ce** livre.*
4 *Elle achète **ces** fruits.*
5 *Elle mange **ce** fruit.*
6 *Il achète **ce** magazine.*
7 *Elle a regardé **ce** film.*
8 *Il a joué au football dans **ce** stade.*
9 *Il a regardé le film dans **ce** cinéma.*
10 *Elle danse dans **cette** discothèque.*

Work in pairs. One should look at **this** page and the other at page 169.

You and your partner will, in turn, play the parts of a TV interview and a star. To begin with, you are the star.

Here are details of your star's life to help you answer your partner's questions:

stage name	*Jacques* (or *Marie*) *Célèbre*
real name	*Jacques* (or *Marie*) *Dupont*
home	*Avignon*
work address	a flat in Paris
taste in music	
taste in food	} you choose
favourite drinks	
recently	recorded *(enregistré)* 'Sans toi' in a studio in Los Angeles
soon	will work on an album *'un 33 tours'* with *Sophie Marsaud*

Now you and your partner can swap roles. Your job is to find out the following information about your star, *Marie* (or *Marcel*) *Daudet:*

1 real name; family details (parents/brothers & sisters)
2 home (where is this?)
3 where does he/she work?
4 musical taste
5 taste in food
6 favourite drinks
7 what she or he has been doing recently?
8 what she or he is going to do in the near future?

Au marché

DIALOGUES

Au marché

Dialogue 1

Cliente	Bonjour, Monsieur. Je cherche un sac à main.
Serveur	Oui…j'en ai beaucoup…quelle couleur voulez-vous?
Cliente	Vous en avez en noir?
Serveur	Oui…en voici…
Cliente	Celui-ci est trop grand…et celui-là est laid…combien coûte celui-ci?
Serveur	Il fait 120 francs, Madame.
Cliente	Il est un peu cher…
Serveur	Eh bien…j'ai celui-ci…
Cliente	Oui…j'aime assez…il fait combien?
Serveur	Il fait 90 francs, Madame.
Cliente	Bien…je le prends.

Dialogue 2

Cliente	Bonjour Monsieur…qu'est-ce que vous avez comme chemises, s'il vous plaît?
Serveur	En quelle taille?
Cliente	C'est pour mon fils…il fait du 38…
Serveur	Regardez dans ce rayon-ci, Madame.
Cliente	Merci, Monsieur.

Dialogue 3

Cliente	Qu'est-ce que vous avez comme fromages bleus, s'il vous plaît?
Serveur	J'ai du bleu de Bresse, Madame, puis du bleu d'Auvergne… du Roquefort…
Cliente	Il est comment votre bleu d'Auvergne…
Serveur	Il est excellent, Madame…essayez un petit bout…

Dialogue 4

Client	Il fait combien, votre beurre, Madame?
Serveuse	14 francs le kilo, Monsieur. Je vous en mets combien?
Client	J'en prendrai une livre.

DIRECTIONS

CRUSTACÉS 15F LE KILO   12F LES 100 GRAMMES

FRUITS DE MER   5F PIÈCE   10F 20 LA LIVRE

LE MARCHÉ AUX PUCES

LE MARCHÉ PONCELET EST OUVERT TOUT L'ÉTÉ

STATIONNEMENT INTERDIT LES JOURS DE MARCHÉ

MARCHÉ COUVERT

4F 50 LA DOUZAINE

B j'écoute

You are going to hear a series of ten people buying various things at different market stalls. In each case, write down, on your copy of the chart below what the customer wants to buy, what quantity is wanted and the final cost of what is bought.

	customer	purchase	quantity	total cost
1				
2				
3				
4				
5				

C trois... deux... un...TOP!

Once again, you have a second or two in which to find some way of answering your French friends' questions! Answer as fast as you can before the bleep!

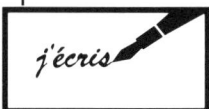

j'écris

1 Write a letter to the tourist office in Bordeaux. You and your family would like to stay near the town for two nights during August. Get information about the region so that you and your family can plan the holiday.

2 Imagine that you are staying with your French penfriend. You are alone in the house when the phone rings. Write a note for your friend saying that Monsieur Brytygier rang to invite the family to spend the day at his house tomorrow. Could your friend's father give him a ring when he comes in?

   Remember that your French does not have to be perfect, but you must get the message across somehow.

3 Write a postcard to a French friend. Use the postcard below for inspiration but don't use too much of it.

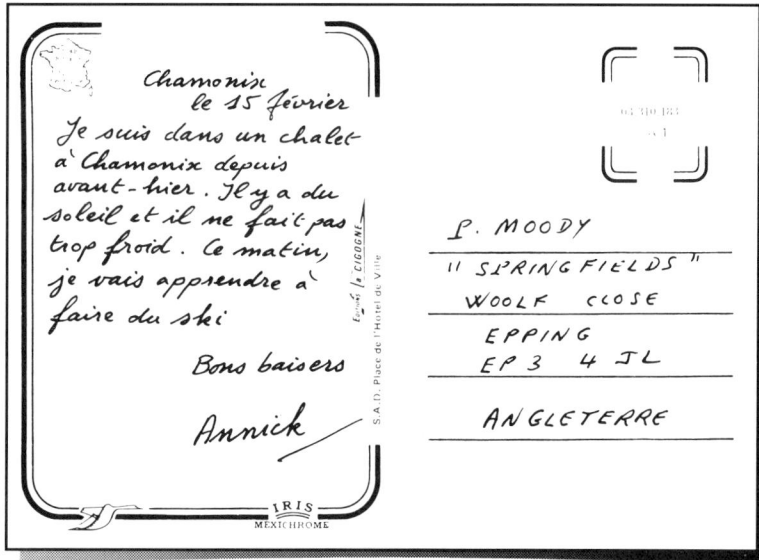

Chamonix
le 15 février
Je suis dans un chalet
à Chamonix depuis
avant-hier. Il y a du
soleil et il ne fait pas
trop froid. Ce matin,
je vais apprendre à
faire du ski

Bons baisers

Annick

P. MOODY
"SPRING FIELDS"
WOOLF CLOSE
EPPING
EP3 4 JL

ANGLETERRE

je cherche

Imagine that following a family holiday to Paris, your mother receives the following letter, and is baffled by it. As the only French speaker in the family, you are asked to help. Do the best you can! If you manage to get any idea at all of what this is about you'll be doing well!

> **Préfecture de police de Paris**
> Bureau des contraventions,
> Ile de la cité,
> 75001 PARIS
>
> le 5 Septembre, 1988
>
> Madame,
>
> Vous voudrez bien trouver ci-joint une contravention relative à une infraction au code de la route. Celle-ci concerne le non respect d'un feu de signalisation à l'angle de l'avenue Georges V et de l'avenue des Champs-Elysées.
>
> Vous êtes priée de faire le nécessaire pour régler la somme de 800 francs dans le delai imparti de 15 jours mentionné au dos de la contravention.
>
> A défaut je serai contraint de prendre contact avec les autorités britanniques.
>
> salutations distinguées,
>   pour le préfet de police, et par délégation,
>   le directeur du service des contraventions,
>
>   Fernand de la Ferté Beaucourt

Où passer les vacances en France? Il y a énormément de possibilités… par exemple, on peut aller à Paris pour regarder les monuments et bâtiments célèbres.

Si vous aimez le sport, vous pouvez faire du ski dans les Alpes au sud-est de la France, ou en Auvergne, au centre de la France.

nord – north	*on peut* – you can (one can)
au nord – in the north	*vous pouvez* – you can
sud – south	*le bâtiment* – the building
est – east	*le soleil* – sun
ouest – west	*la mer* – sea
centre – centre	*la côte* – coast
où – where	*coûte* – costs

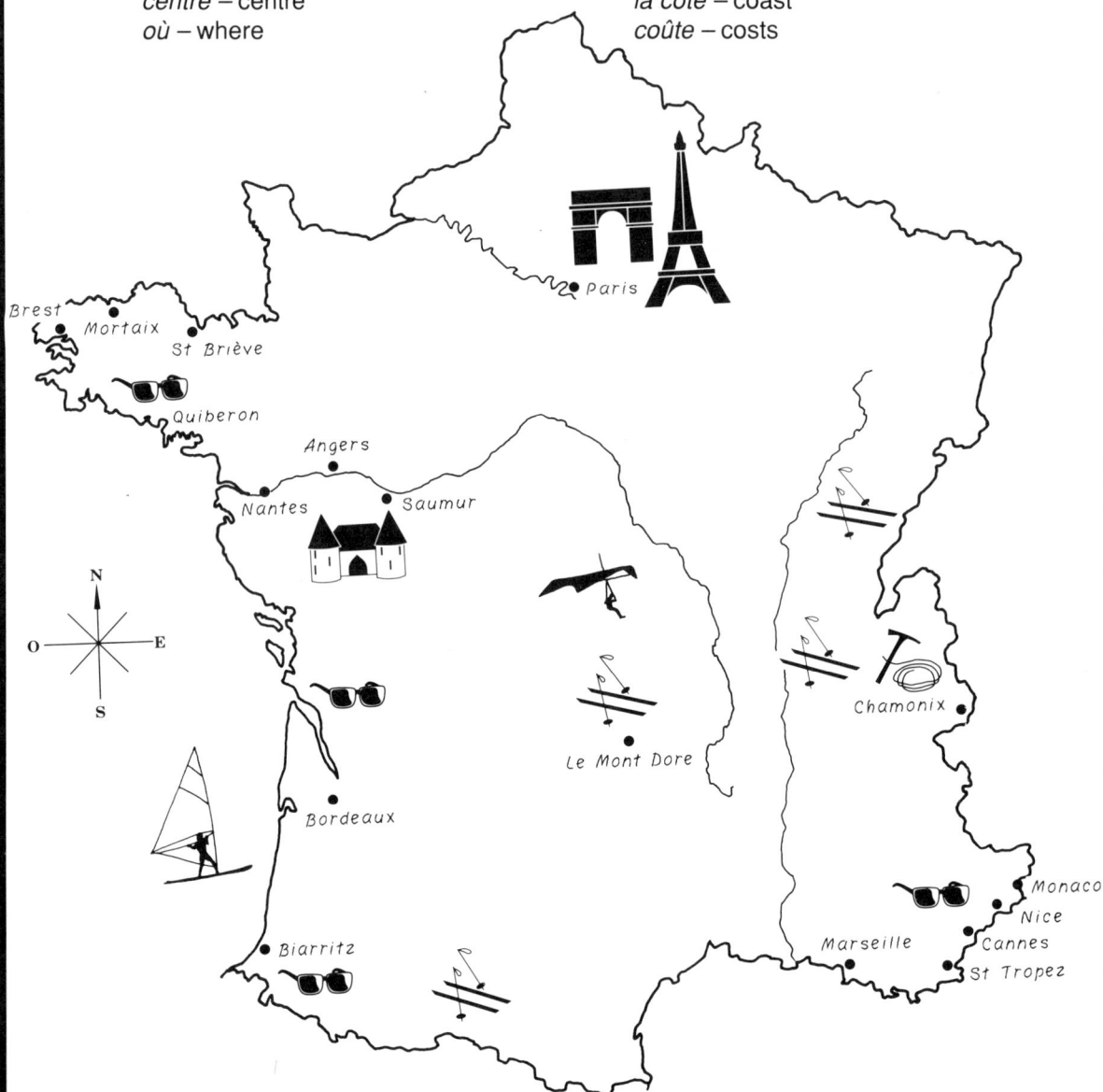

Si vous aimez le soleil et la mer, vous pouvez aller sur la côte méditerranéenne, à Nice, à Cannes et à Saint Tropez… mais attention… ça coûte cher!

You should be able to:

1 ask for a particular size or colour of item;

2 say what your size is in shoes or clothing;

3 say how long you've been doing something;

4 say who did something or had something done to them;

5 make it clear which person or thing you are talking about.

RÉPERTOIRE

Au marché

un marché	market
une rue	road
une ville	town
une caravane	caravan
une camionnette	van
une cassette	cassette
un poisson	fish
cher	expensive
bon marché	cheap
les vêtements	clothes
les sous-vêtements	underclothes
le slip	pants
le maillot de corps	vest
la taille	size (clothes)
la pointure	size (shoes)
une poule	hen
un canard	duck
un lapin	rabbit

j'écris

Write a letter to an imaginary French correspondent:

1 introduce yourself (you're writing to her or him for the first time);

2 talk about your family;

3 talk about your friends;

4 say what you enjoy doing, mention your hobbies and sporting interests;

5 talk about your likes and dislikes.

You'll find a lot of material to help you in *Leçon 1* and also in *Leçon 6*, which deals with letter-writing.

Expressions utiles

J'aime	nager.	I like	swimming.
J'aime	monter à cheval.	I like	horse-riding
Je m'intéresse à	la photographie.	I'm interested in	photography.
Je collectionne	les timbres.	I collect	stamps.
Je suis	pêcheur.	I am	a fisherman.

Your teacher will tell you how to say what your particular interest is in French.

Entertainment and sport

Le café

The café is a place of entertainment rather like the English pub; the atmosphere there is very different, however. In a café you can buy drinks, snacks, sometimes meals and you'll often find a jukebox, pinball machines, table football and arcade electronic games.

If you are under 16, you'll need to be accompanied by an adult and laws governing who can drink alcohol are similar to those in this country.

Often, especially in Paris, cafés charge different prices according to where you sit. The cheapest place to drink will be at the bar; the next cheapest place will be sitting at a table inside, while the most expensive part of the café will be *la terrasse*, the seats outside the café on the pavement.

Here are some of the drinks which you might like to order in a café:

un café	coffee (this will be served black)	*un citron pressé*	lemon squash (fresh)
un crème, café crème	white coffee	*une menthe à l'eau*	mint drink
		une grenadine	pomegranate juice
un thé citron	lemon tea	*une eau minérale*	mineral water
un thé au lait	tea with milk	*une limonade*	lemonade
un chocolat chaud	hot chocolate		

je lis

Dans un café on peut boire de l'alcool (de la bière, du vin, etc.), mais on peut boire du café, du thé, du chocolat chaud et bien d'autres boissons non-alcoolisées aussi. Dans ce café, derrière le comptoir il y a une machine à café.

Sur cette photo on voit la terrasse et l'intérieur d'un café. Devant le café il y a un grand parking. C'est l'heure du déjeuner. Ces gens ont mangé et sont venus boire un bon café avant de retourner au travail.

Here are some typical café snacks:

un croque-monsieur	bread, cheese, ham, toasted
un croque-madame	as above, but with fried egg
un oeuf dur	hard-boiled egg
une quiche lorraine	ham and egg pie
une pizza	pizza
un sandwich	a sandwich, usually made out of a stick loaf

Expressions utiles

le juke box	juke box
le babyfoot	table football (very different from ours as the men can easily trap the ball, so other techniques are used – practise before you take on the locals!)
le jeu électronique	arcade electronic game
le flipper	pinball machine

Quiz

Can you guess what this is?
The machine is used in French cafés.

Answer on page 158

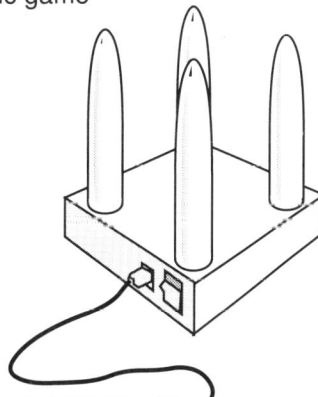

Le cinéma

On a rainy day you may decide you'd like to go to the cinema. It's often possible to see a film in English, especially in Paris.

You need to examine the cinema programme (in Paris, there are two magazines which give a lot of information about these: *Pariscope* and *L'officiel des spectacles*).

Of course, you may decide to watch a film that's in French. If you do, it might be wise to go for an action film. There is some information in this photo which may save you money. Can you read it?

le billet

le film

la sortie

le guichet

Look out for these abbreviations:

VO	version originale	film in original language, but probably with sub-titles
VF	version française	film dubbed into French
VA	version anglaise	film dubbed into English

Expressions utiles

interdit aux moins de…ans	no one under…may view the film
il est interdit de fumer	no smoking – this is usual in French cinemas and theatres
sous-titré	sub-titled
l'ouvreuse	usherette
la salle	auditorium
le balcon	balcony

Au cinéma

Je voudrais	une place deux places	pour	.... la salle	une deux trois etc.	s'il vous plaît.

The film title goes in the space.

je révise je révise je révise You'll notice that cinema guides often mention the country of origin of the film. This seems to be a good moment to remind you of how to use these nationality words:

country	language	people	a film from there
Angleterre or la Grande Bretagne	anglais	les Anglais les Britanniques	anglais britannique
France	français	les Français	français
Allemagne	allemand	les Allemands	allemand
Amérique (les États-Unis)	anglais	les Américains	américain
Espagne	espagnol	les Espagnols	espagnol
Italie	italien	les Italiens	italien
la Russie (l'USSR)	russe	les Russes	russe or soviétique

How to talk about a film you've seen

C'était	un western. un dessin animé. un film de science fiction. un film policier. un film de guerre. un film d'épouvante.	It was	a western. a cartoon. a science fiction film. a detective film. a war film. a horror film.

C'était Le film était	bon. mauvais. très mauvais. un navet. intéressant. ennuyeux. pas mal. comme ci comme ça.	It was The film was	good. bad. very bad. rubbish. interesting. boring. not bad. so so.

je cherche

1 Find two films that you think you'd like to see.

2 Check that they're in English.

3 Note down the name of the cinema.

1 Where could you see the Star Wars trilogy with an English soundtrack?

2 What advantage would there be in watching all three films?

UGC NORMANDIE (v.o.)
GRAND REX (v.f. 70 m/m)
UGC MONTPARNASSE (v.f.)

Pour les 3 films : Tarif réduit
Pour 1 film : Plein tarif

LA SAGA DE
LA GUERRE DES ETOILES

GUERRE ÉTOILES

L'EMPIRE CONTRE-ATTAQUE
DES ETOILES

LA GUERRE DES ETOILES
LE RETOUR DU JEDI

GAITE BOULEVARD, 25, bd Poissonnière, 45.08.96.45, M° Montmartre. Perm. 13h à 24h. Ven., sam., séance suppl. à 24h. Pl. : 20 F :
1) **RUNAWAY TRAIN** et **ATTENTION LES DEGATS.**

2) **LA MACHINE A DECOUDRE** et **LES RATS DE MANHATTAN.**

GAUMONT OPERA, 31, bd des Italiens, 47.42.60.33, M° Opéra. Perm. de 14h à 24h. Pl. : 31 F. TR 20 F : lundi et — de 18 ans et + de 60 ans du dim. 20h au mar. 19h. Etud. et C.V. de lundi au ven. 18h.
1) Séances : 13h40, 16h15, 18h50, 21h25. Film 20 mn après :
△ **37 DEGRES 2 LE MATIN**

2) Séances : 14h, 19h30. Film 30 mn après :
IL ETAIT UNE FOIS EN AMERIQUE (vo)

3) Séances : 13h50, 15h50, 17h50, 18h05, 20h10, 22h15. Film 20 mn après :
LE DEBUTANT

4) Séances : 13h45, 17h20, 20h55. Film 15 mn après :
BARRY LYNDON

5) Séances : 14h, 16h05, 18h10, 20h15, 22h20. Film 15 mn après :
▢ **L'EMPIRE DES SENS**

6) Séances : 14h20, 17h30, 20h40. Film 20 mn après (Pl. : 35 F, réd. : 24 F.)
OUT OF AFRICA (Dolby stéréo)

GAUMONT RICHELIEU, 27, bd Poissonnière, 42.33.56.70, M° Rue-Montmartre. Pl. : 30 F. TR 20 F : Lundi et moins de 18 ans, + de 60 ans, du dim. au mar. 19h C.V. du lun. au ven. jusqu'à 18h.
1) Séances : 13h50, 15h55, 18H, 20h05, 22h10. Film 20 mn après :
△ **HITCHER**

2) Séances : 14h15, 16h40, 19h05, 21h30. Film 20 mn après :
JAMES BOND CONTRE Dr NO

3) Séances : 13h45, 15h50, 18h, 20h05, 22h15. Film 10 mn après :
LE CONTRAT

4) Séances : 13h50, 15h50, 17h55, 19h55, 22h. Film 20 mn après :
BLACK MIC MAC

5) Séances : 13h45, 15h50, 17h55, 20h05, 22h10. Film 15 mn après :
PROFESSION : GENIE

IMPERIAL PATHE, 29, bd des Italiens, 47.42.72.52, M° Opéra. (H). Pl. : 32 F. TR 22 F : lundi et — de 18 ans + de 60 ans du dim. 20h au mar. 19h et étud. du mar. au ven. jusqu'à 18h30.
1) Séance : 13h55, 16h, 18h05, 20h10, 22h15. Film 15 mn après :
△ **LE DIABLE AU CORPS** de Bellocchio

O **ROCKY N°3 L'ŒIL DU TIGRE (L')** (Rocky III) (Eye of the tiger). — Amér., coul. (82). Film de boxe, de Sylvester Stallone : Rocky Balboa relève un nouveau défi... Avec Sylvester Stallone, Talia Shire, Carl Weathers, Burgess Meredith. Rex 2°, Ermitage 8° (vo), UGC Gobelins 13°, Miramar 14°, Images 18°.

M **ROMEO ET JULIETTE.** — Brit., coul. (66). Film-ballet, de Paul Czinner : La tragédie de William Shakespeare transposée en ballet par le musicien russe Serge Prokofiev. Avec Rudy Noureev, Margot Fonteyn, David Blair, Desmond Doyle, la troupe du « Royal Ballet de Londres » et l'orchestre du « Royal Opera House Covent Garden ». (Voir rubrique « Nouveaux films »).

O **ROSE BONBON (Pretty in Pink).** — Amér., coul. (85). Comédie dramatique, de Howard Deutch : Une lycéenne de condition modeste s'éprend d'un de ses camarades, jeune « richard ». Avec Molly Ringwald, Harry Dean Stanton, Jon Cryer, Annie Potts. George V 8° (vo).

C **ROSE POURPRE DU CAIRE (LA)** (The Purple Rose of Cairo). — Amér., coul. (85). Comédie, de Woody Allen : Une jeune fille passionnée de cinéma rencontre le héros de ses rêves. Avec Mia Farrow, Jeff Daniels, Danny Aiello, Irving Metzman. Studio de la Harpe 5° (vo).

A **RUNAWAY TRAIN.** — Amér., coul. (85). Aventure dramatique, d'Andrei Konchalovsky : Deux évadés, en Alaska, par une température de — 50 degrés, empruntent un convoi ferroviaire dont les freins vont lâcher... Avec John Voight, Eric Roberts, Rebecca DeMornay, Kyle T. Heffner. Gaîté Boulevard 2°, Elysées Lincoln 8° (vo), 7 Parnassiens 14° (vo).

D **SACRIFICE (LE).** — Franco-suédois, coul. (86). Drame psychologique, d'Andrei Tarkovski : Pour un homme, un sacrifice — celui de sa propre vie — qui s'avère indispensable dans le monde d'aujourd'hui privé de spiritualité. Avec Erland Josephson, Susan Fleetwood, Valérie Mairesse, Allan Edwall. Saint-André-des-Arts 6° (vo), Pagode 7° (vo).

D **SALVADOR.** — Amér., coul. (85). Drame, d'Oliver Stone : Trois Américains témoins de la guerre au Salvador. Un film courageux sur le dangereux métier de reporter de guerre d'après la véritable histoire de Richard Boyle. Avec James Woods, Jim Belushi, John Savage. Triomphe 8° (vo).

C **SHOP AROUND THE CORNER (THE).** — Amér., noir et blanc (40). Comédie, de Ernst Lubitsch : Un couple, amoureux par correspondance (sans s'être jamais rencontré) se déteste dans la vie. Avec James Stewart, Margaret Sullavan, Frank Morgan, Joseph Schildkraut. Action Christine 6° (vo).

H ▢ **SIBERIADE (Siberiada).** — Soviétique, coul. (77-79). Epopée, d'Andrei Mikhalkov-Kontchalovski : Une vaste fresque de la vie en Sibérie, du début de ce siècle à 1965. Avec Wladimir Samailov, Vitali Solomina, Natalia Andreitchenko, Serguei Salhourov. Cosmos 6° (vo), Triomphe 8°.

**UGC BIARRITZ - REX - UGC BOULEVARD - UGC DANTON
UGC MONTPARNASSE - UGC GOBELINS - UGC CONVENTION - MISTRAL
NATION - 3 SECRETAN - GARE DE LYON - FORUM LES HALLES
ST-LAZARE PASQUIER - LES IMAGES - MAILLOT
et dans les salles de la périphérie**

ALAIN SARDE présente
MICHEL BOUJENAH

VALERIE STEFFEN   KARIM ALLAOUI
VINCENT LINDON   MICHEL AUMONT

Grunelle Blues

JACQUES OTMEZGUINE

> *Qu'est ce qu'on fait ce soir?*

Dialogue 1

Garçon	Messieurs-dames?
Cliente	Je prendrai un Orangina...et vous?
2ᵉ client	Pour moi, ce sera un crème...
3ᵉ client	Et pour moi un citron pressé.
Garçon	Alors...un Orangina, un crème et un citron pressé.

Dialogue 2

Garçon	Messieurs-dames, qu'est-ce que je vous sers?
Client	Je prendrai un demi, et puis un croque-monsieur.
Garçon	Oui...
2ᵉ client	Et moi, je prendrai un Coca et un oeuf dur...
Garçon	Alors...un demi, un Coca, un croque-monsieur et un oeuf dur...

Dialogue 3

Cliente	Deux places pour 'Prunelle blues', s'il vous plaît.
Employé	Ah, je suis désolé, Mademoiselle, mais c'est complet.

Dialogue 4

Client	Bonjour, Madame...deux places pour 'Lawrence d'Arabie', s'il vous plaît.
Employée	Oui...voilà...cela vous fait cinquante francs.
Client	C'est quelle salle, Madame?
Employée	C'est la salle trois, Monsieur.

Dialogue 5

Cliente	Bonjour, Monsieur.
Employé	Bonjour, Mademoiselle.
Cliente	Deux places pour 'Rocky 22', s'il vous plaît.
Employé	Quarante francs, s'il vous plaît.
Cliente	Où est-ce qu'on peut acheter des confiseries, s'il vous plaît?
Employé	À l'entrée, Mademoiselle.

Activités en plein air

En France on peut faire beaucoup d'activités en plein air. Par exemple, la planche à voile est très populaire en ce moment.

Voici une boutique spécialisée: elle vend des planches à voile mais elle les loue aussi. Si tu veux, tu peux y louer une planche à voile.

Expressions utiles

Ça coûte combien pour louer …, s'il vous plaît?　　How much does it cost to hire a …?

Je voudrais louer…,s'il vous plaît.　　I would like to hire …

À la maison

Les micro-ordinateurs sont très populaires en France. Les Français achètent les ordinateurs Amstrad, Atari, Commodore… mais aussi des machines françaises comme l'ordinateur Thomson TO-O7.

La vidéo est aussi très populaire comme distraction: cette photo, prise à l'intérieur d'un grand supermarché, montre le rayon vidéo.

Can you work out exactly what you get for 3990F, 9990F or 11990F?

ENTREZ DANS LE MONDE DE L'ATARI ST

avec **RUN** l'authentique spécialiste d'atari

INFORMATIQUE

2 MAGASINS RUN est ouvert le dimanche 21 décembre de 10 à 19 heures!!!

62, rue Gérard - 75013 PARIS
Tél.: (1) 45.81.51.44 - Télex : RUNINFO 270641 F
Ouvert du lundi au samedi de 9 h à 19 h
Métro : PLACE D'ITALIE

7, rue de l'Eglise - 92200 NEUILLY-SUR-SEINE
Tél.: (1) 46.40.73.26 nouveau
Ouvert du lundi au samedi de 10 h à 19 h
Métro et Bus : PONT DE NEUILLY - Sortie Rue de l'Eglise

16/32 bits **la puissance révélée** ▶

la micro plaisir

RAPIDITÉ ET PUISSANCE

520 STF
Ordinateur personnel 520 STF
+ lecteur de disquette 3" 1/2
intégré 500 Ko
+ câble PERITEL
Prix : 3990 F

icônes

1040 STF monochrome ▶
ordinateur professionnel
+ lecteur de disquette 1 Mo intégré
+ moniteur monochrome SM 124
Prix : 9990 F

sous GEM

souris

1040 STF couleur
Ordinateur professionnel
+ lecteur de disquette 1 Mo intégré
+ moniteur couleur SC 1224
Prix : 11.990 F

menus déroulants

		COMPTANT		CRÉDIT CÉTÉLEM			
1	520 STF	3990 F TTC	340.20 F par mois 12 mensualités	Apport comptant 390 F	TEG 18,24 %	Coût total du crédit avec assurance 482.40 F	
2	1040 STFM monochrome	9990 F TTC	814.30 F par mois 12 mensualités	Apport comptant 1390 F	TEG 18,24 %	Coût total du crédit avec assurance 1171.80 F	
3	1040 STFC couleur	11990 F TTC	948.10 F par mois 12 mensualités	Apport comptant 1990 F	TEG 18,24 %	Coût total du crédit avec assurance 1377.20 F	

DIRECTIONS

VESTIAIRE

SNACKS À TOUTE HEURE

Location de patins à glace

BOISSONS

N'avez vous rien oublié?

Réduction accordée sur présentation d'une carte d'étudiant

TARIF RÉDUIT LE LUNDI

Protection des mineurs et répression de l'ivresse publique

Séance à 14H00 : Film à 14H30

Les jeux sont interdits aux enfants de moins de 16 ans non-accompagnés

BOISSONS PILOTES

5 SALLES AIR-CONDITIONNÉ : SON DOLBY

B
j'écoute

You are going to hear a series of ten people ordering drinks for themselves and for friends in a café. The numbers of people wanting drinks will vary from order to order, of course. Fill in the drinks ordered on your copy of the chart below.

	drinks ordered
1	
2	

Le sport

It is easy to talk about sport in French because the words for sports are **usually** the same as ours (although they are occasionally shortened) and they are *le* words (masculine).

Here are some popular sports:

le basket	le football (le foot)	le golf	le hockey
le judo	le karaté	le ski	
le rugby	le tennis	le volley	

Some sports do get different names in French:

la boxe	boxing	le catch	wrestling
le deltaplane	hang-gliding	la planche à voile	windsurfing
la natation	swimming	le patin à glace	ice-skating
la gymnastique	gymnastics	le cyclisme	cycling
le ski nautique	water skiing	le billard	billiards
la pétanque	French bowls	le surf	surfing

Someone may ask you what sport you do or like:

> *Qu'est-ce que tu fais comme sport?*
> What sport do you do?
>
> *Qu'est-ce que tu aimes comme sport?*
> What sport do you like?

You can answer, for example:

> *J'aime bien le rugby.* I like rugby.
>
> *Je fais du hockey.* I play hockey.
>
> *Je joue au hockey.* I play hockey.

trois... C
deux...
un...TOP!

Once again, you have a second or two in which to find some way of answering the question! You and your French friend are in a café. It will help to have page 149 in front of you. Answer as fast as you can before the bleep!

j'écris

1   Write a letter to the Hotel International in Nice. You and your family would like to stay there for two nights on the 15th and 16th July. Make it clear what rooms you want and whether or not you want a bath or a shower in each. Ask if the hotel is near the beach.

2   Write out the phrase used to sign off a formal letter, then check that you've got it right! If you've made a mistake, write it out again!

3   Write a postcard to a friend in France who has just sent you this card in which they complain about their holiday:

VICHY (Allier)
Santé - détente - vacances
Le lac d'Allier - Au premier plan,
le bateau promenade "Pierre Coulon"

Vichy le 23 avril

*Je suis dans une auberge
de jeunesse près d'un
lac à Vichy. On n'a pas
beaucoup de chance
parce qu'il pleut depuis
trois jours. Je joue aux
cartes toute la journée
C'est ennuyeux*

Je vous embrasse

Françoise

03.310.81

N. WRIGHT
9a BELGRAVE ROAD
EASTBOURNE
E. SUSSEX
EA3 4TQ
ANGLETERRE

IRIS

4 Whilst on holiday in France, you met a boy (or a girl) and got on very well with him or her… He or she is now writing to you to tell you about a trip to England next month. This would normally be good news, but unfortunately there is now someone else! Write back! Try to be kind.

Lescheraines, le 15 août

Chère Tracy (cher Brian)

Je suis très triste depuis que tu es parti (e). Je retourne souvent au café où je t'ai rencontré (e) pour la première fois. Je joue aux cartes avec les copains (copines), mais cela ne m'amuse pas. Tu me manques énormément.

Mais j'ai une bonne nouvelle à t'annoncer : le mois prochain, je vais aller en Angleterre ! Est-ce que je peux te rendre visite à Chipping Sodbury ?

Je t'embrasse bien fort

Dominique

je lis

Can you work out why this viewer is complaining to the TV magazine *Télé-poche*?

Le Courrier

DYNASTIE SUR M6 : LA FRANCE GRONDE

« Dynastie », c'est fini, en tout cas sur FR3. Ça reprendra sur M6 en septembre. Je suis une fan inconditionnelle de ce feuilleton et je vous demande, et surtout à FR3, de continuer à passer cette série américaine, il faut que ça continue ! Tout simplement parce que j'habite en province et nous ne pourrons recevoir M6 avant 2 ans. Alors que faire ?

Séverine X,
Loir-et-Cher

Work in pairs. One of you should look at **this** page and the other at page 170.
You and your partner will take it in turns to play the parts of a waiter and customer in a café in France.

For the first game, you are the waiter.

Below is a list of the drinks and snacks sold at the café, together with the prices:

boissons		snacks	
thé (nature)	8F	croque-monsieur	21F
thé (au citron)	8F 50	oeuf dur	6F
café	6F	sandwich au jambon	10F
café crème (grand)	7F 50	sandwich au fromage	15F 50
café crème (petit)	5F 50	sandwich au pâté	14F
Orangina	9F		
Coca-Cola	9F		
menthe à l'eau	15F		
bière à la pression	10F		
bière en bouteille	12F		

Bear in mind that:

1 You've run out of Coca-Cola

2 You've got strict instructions not to sell any alcoholic drinks to minors, so watch out for English tourists who may try it on.

It's now your turn to play the part of the customer.

In fact, you play the part of the only person in a group of tourists who speaks French, so you have to order for everyone at your table.

Each of the five people in your party wants something to eat and something to drink.

One person wants tea in the British way, with milk, so try to arrange this. Another wants three hard-boiled eggs. A third finds that the coffee is cold (le café est froid), so you try to sort out the problem with the waiter.

You should now be able to:

1 order a drink in a café;

2 order a snack in a café;

3 be able to read a cinema programme and choose a suitable film;

4 say what you thought of a film afterwards;

5 say where a film comes from and what language it is in.

Ce monsieur montre des vélos miniatures aux passants dans une rue à Vichy (voir aussi la page 54). Les enfants aiment bien ces petits vélos.

RÉPERTOIRE

Le café

un café	coffee
un crème	white coffee
un thé	tea
le citron	lemon
le lait	milk
un chocolat	chocolate
un citron pressé	lemon (fresh)
une menthe à l'eau	mint drink
une grenadine	pomegranate juice
une eau minérale	mineral water
une limonade	lemonade
de l'alcool	alcohol
des boissons alcoolisées	alcoholic drinks
un croque-monsieur	toasted sandwich
un oeuf dur	hard-boiled egg
le babyfoot	table football
le jeu	game
le flipper	pinball machine

Le cinéma

un film	film
un billet	ticket
une salle	auditorium
le guichet	booking office
la sortie	exit
une place	a seat
un western	western
un dessin animé	cartoon
un film de science fiction	a science fiction film
un film policier	cops & robbers
un film de guerre	war film
un film d'épouvante	horror film

Opinions

bon	good
mauvais	bad
un navet	awful (a turnip)
intéressant	interesting
ennuyeux	boring
pas mal	not bad
comme ci comme ça	so so

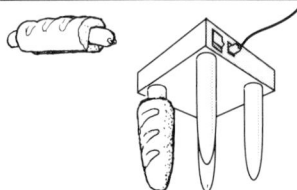

It's a hot-dog machine for French stick loaves.

Answer to page 147 Quiz

For this game you will need the six descriptions of tourists which appear below. Your job is to get your partner to let all of the tourists through her or his frontier post checkpoint.

The description with a star next to it is that of a jewel thief and you must try to get the thief through the checkpoint as well!

Your partner has a rough idea of the thief's identity but she or he can only ask each one four questions, because she or he can't afford to let innocent tourists be kept hanging around. You need to choose the right moment to send the jewel thief through; you must answer the questions she or he asks according to the details given below.

Tourists (you can make them men or women)

1 *Dupont*
   Âge: 31 ans
   1 frère (Pierre)
   1 soeur (Marie)
   Son père est banquier
   Sa mère est informaticienne

2 *Durand*
   Âge: 32 ans
   1 frère (Jean)
   1 soeur (Marie)
★ *Son père est banquier*
   Sa mère est informaticienne

3 *Dupont*
   Âge: 32 ans
   1 frère (Jean)
   1 soeur (Louise)
   Son père est banquier
   Sa mère est mécanicienne

4 *Dumeil*
   Âge: 33 ans
   1 soeur (Marie)
   Son père est banquier
   Sa mère est informaticienne

5 *Dutheil*
   Âge: 32 ans
   1 frère (Jean)
   Son père est fermier
   Sa mère est informaticienne

6 *Durand*
   Âge: 32 ans
   1 frère (Jean)
   2 soeurs (Marie et Alice)
   Son père est professeur
   Sa mère est informaticienne

informaticienne – computer technician

You are going to play the parts of six customers who are booking into the Hôtel de Paris in Cholet. Below are the things that your hotel guests want, or do not want. Each moon sign represents one night.

Note the mood of each customer given in each box.

Below the illustration are a few phrases which you may find useful.

1

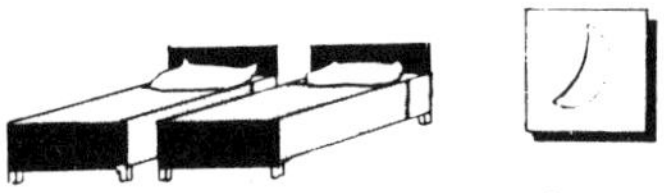

pleasant

2

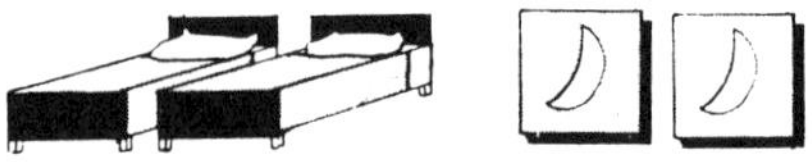

tired

3

in a hurry

4

not very bright

5

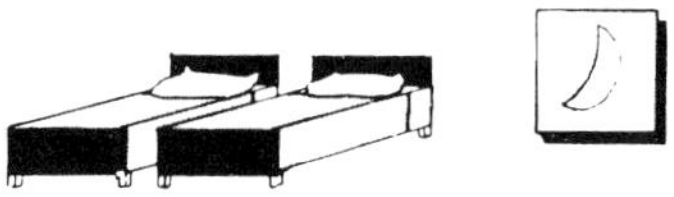

angry

6

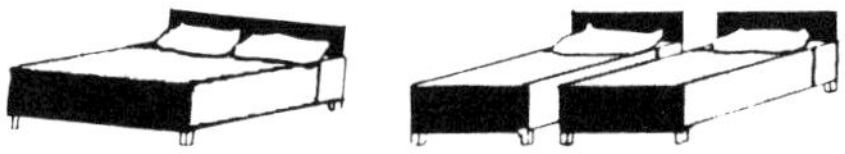

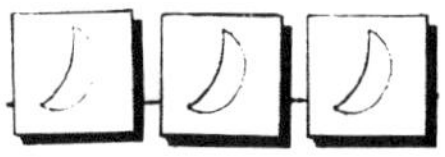

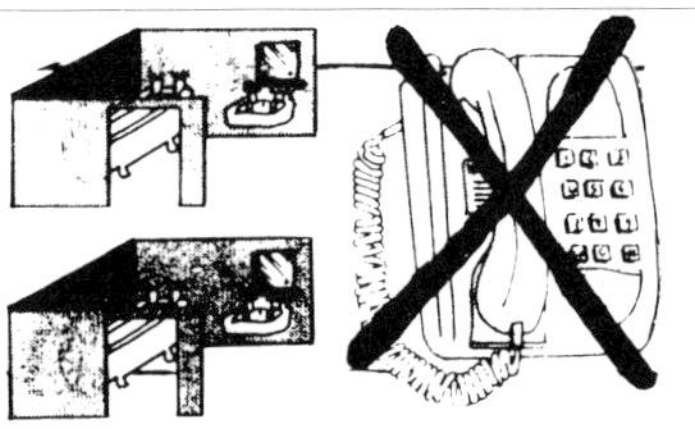

pleasant at first

je voudrais – I would like
je suis pressé – I am in a hurry

je ne veux pas de – I don't want a …
enlevez – take away (here: remove the telephone from the room)

JEU DE RÔLES

Leçon 3

You are the waitress or waiter in a restaurant. Your partner is a customer. She or he is choosing from a menu like the one below but yours is the up-to-date one so warn her or him of any price changes.

On a scrap of paper (or in your exercise book), note your customer's order.

In the three boxes below are listed some other changes which you'll need to tell your customer about if she or he chooses the items mentioned there.

1 These dishes are no longer available:

melon au porto
oeufs mayonnaise
poulet fermière (instead you can offer *steak tartare* or *côtes de porc*)
omelette aux champignons (instead you can offer *gratin dauphinois* or *escalope de veau*)

Expressions utiles

je suis désolé I'm very sorry
on n'a plus de… we haven't got any more…

2 A new version of the menu is being printed with the words:

La maison n'accepte pas les chèques

3 Drinks available:

Bordeaux
  25F la bouteille
  15F la demi-bouteille
Champigny
  20F la bouteille
Orangina 8F
Coca 9F

When you finish, turn to page 40 and play the other part.

ENTRÉES		
1	melon au porto	15F
2	oeufs mayonnaise	15F
3	assiette anglaise	20F
4	escargots de Bourgogne	~~35F~~ 45F

PLATS PRINCIPAUX		
5	poulet fermière	35F
6	côte d'agneau provençale	~~40F~~ 45F
7	truite aux amandes	45F
8	omelette aux champignons	25F

FROMAGES		
9	le camembert	10F
10	le gruyère	10F
11	le roquefort	~~15F~~ 20F
12	le brie	10F

DESSERTS		
13	une salade de fruits	15F
14	un flan au caramel	10F
15	une tarte de saison	~~10F~~ 15F
16	une glace	10F

You are the salesperson in a grocery store.

Your partner has come in with a shopping list and will buy several things from you. Here are the things you sell, together with the prices.

Don't sell any milk as it's gone off *(le lait a tourné)*.

When you finish, turn to page 51 and play the other part.

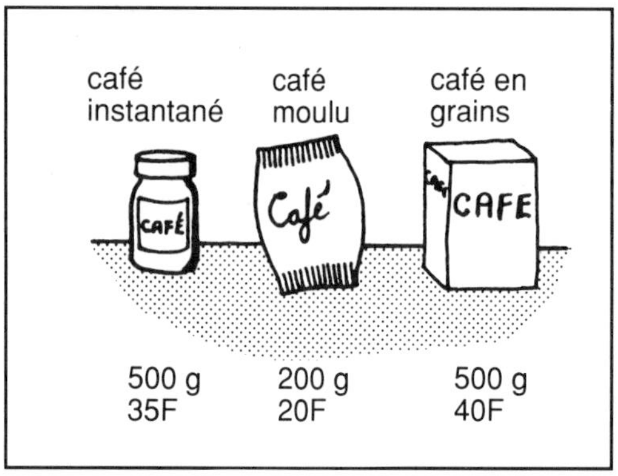

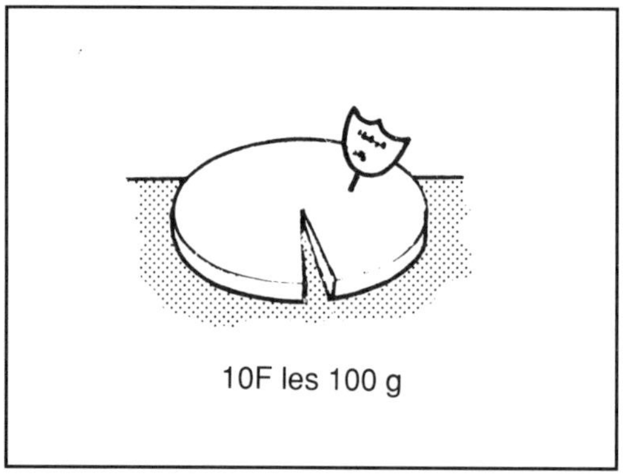

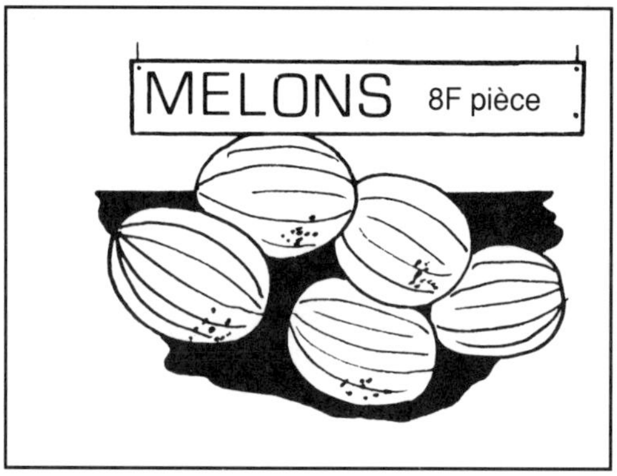

café instantané   café moulu   café en grains

500 g   200 g   500 g
35F   20F   40F

10F les 100 g

MELONS   8F pièce

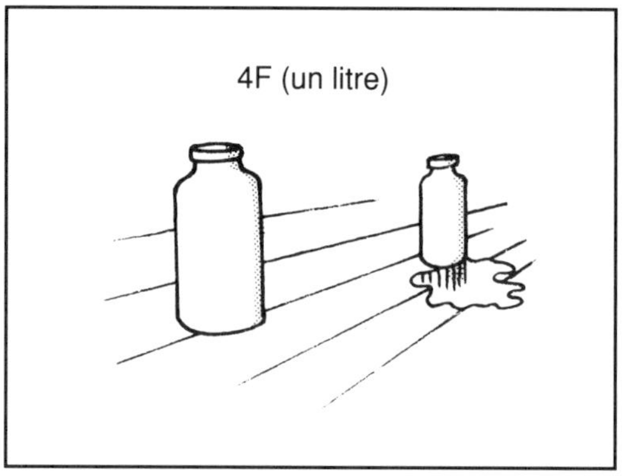

4F (un litre)

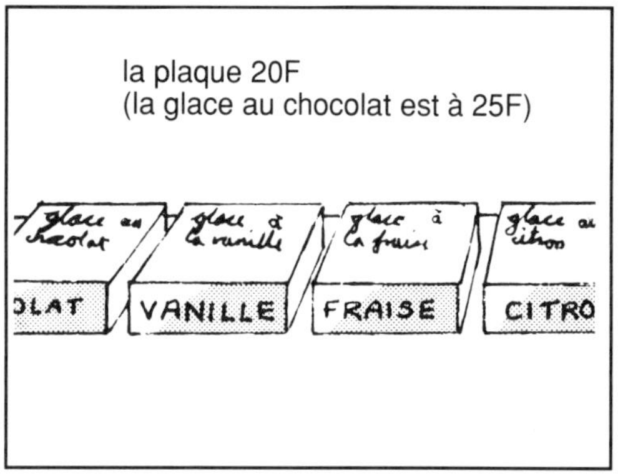

la plaque 20F
(la glace au chocolat est à 25F)

glace au chocolat   glace à la vanille   glace à la fraise   glace au citron

OLAT   VANILLE   FRAISE   CITRO

12F

L'EXPRESS   L'EXPRESS

café instantané – instant coffee
café en grains – coffee beans
café moulu – ground coffee

In this game your partner is visiting a French town. She or he will want to find the way to the places marked on your map. Give her or him directions as if you were standing where the two people are.

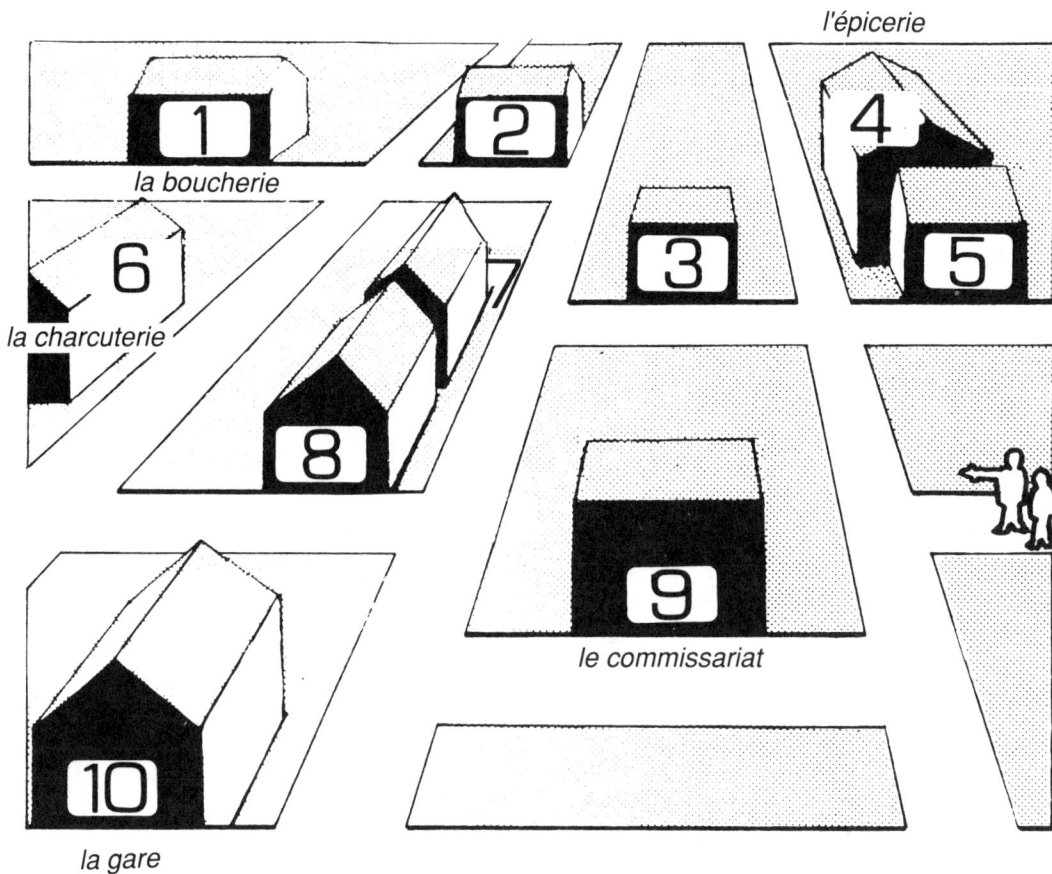

l'épicerie

la boucherie

la charcuterie

le commissariat

la gare

Now you are the visitor in a French town and you must ask your partner how to get to the places shown below and write down the numbers that correspond to them:

the bank
the supermarket
the butcher
the hardware store
the chemist

You are a business customer bringing the firm's mail to the post office. Your mail is for the places shown below.

Your boss told you that the bill should come to 112F assuming that all mail is sent first class.

Make sure you're not overcharged, or your boss will not be pleased!

By the way, you also want to post a few items of personal mail (shown in the last box below). You have to pay for your private correspondence yourself, which comes to 18F 50.

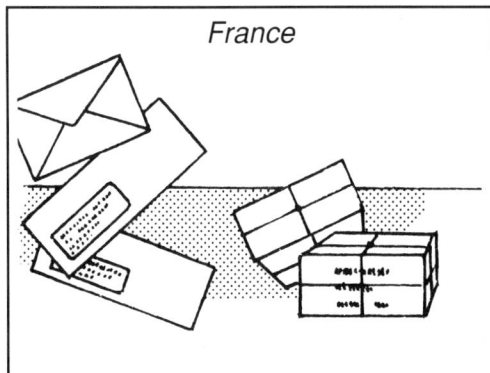

France

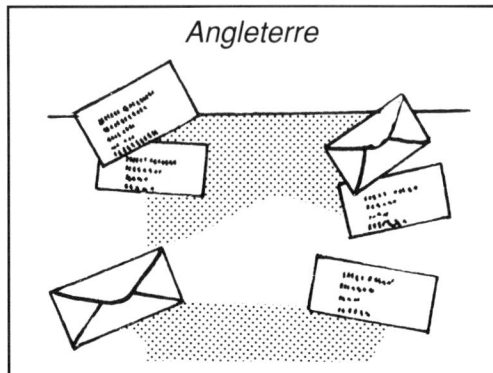

Angleterre

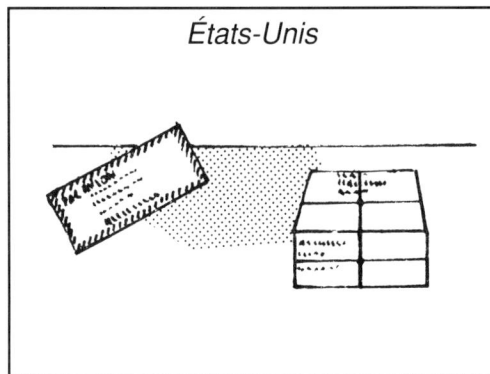

États-Unis

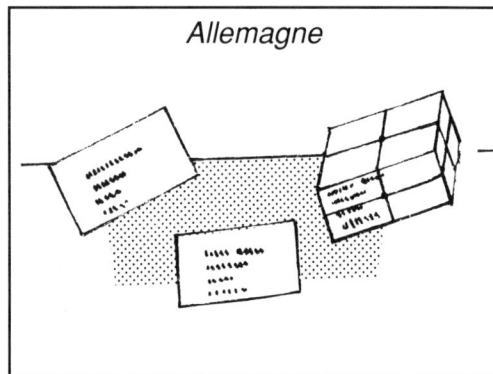

Allemagne

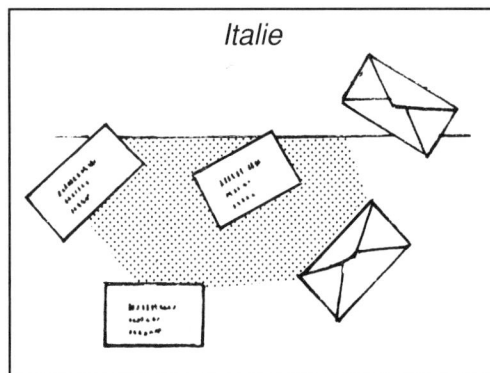

Italie

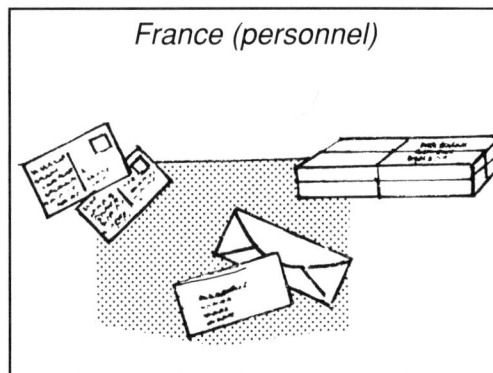

France (personnel)

When you finish, turn to page 73 and play the other part.

You are the ticket salesperson and reservations clerk at various main line rail stations in Paris (only one at a time!).

Your job is to sell tickets and make reservations...and also to answer passengers' questions about their journeys.

The following information will help you do this:

1 Trains to Bordeaux are being delayed by *(ont un retard de)* 20 minutes.

2 While you are a ticket salesperson, refer all requests for information about train times and platforms to the *bureau des renseignements* and for reservations to the *bureau des réservations (adressez-vous au bureau…)*.

3 Tell passengers for Annecy, if need be, that there is no first class accommodation on the trains.

When you finish, turn to page 96 and play the other part.

RENSEIGNEMENTS

Destination	Départs	Prix aller simple		Prix aller et retour		Quai	Observations
		1e	2e	1e	2e		
AIX-LES-BAINS	13h15 ; 15h10	361	241	722	482	1	C R
AMIENS	12h12	97	65	194	130	3	R
ANNECY	14h50 ; 15h50	396	264	792	528	1	R
BOURGES	11h30 ; 16h10	165	108	329	216	2	C
BORDEAUX	16h20 ; 19h15	373	249	746	498	1	C R
CHARTRES	13h13 ; 15h13	69	46	138	92	14	R
LYON	14h35 ; 16h35	333	222	666	444	3	C R
RENNES	14h10 ; 15h10	250	167	500	334	2	R

SERVICES INTERNATIONAUX

BRUXELLES	20h50	NC	NC	NC	NC	1	C R
LONDRES	21h00	NC	NC	NC	720	16	C
MOSCOU	20h30	NC	NC	NC	NC	14	C R

NC: non-communiqué
C: il faut changer de train
R: restauration

Answer the questions your partner asks you about where you went on the days or during the periods shown.

You will have to say how you travelled and what time you arrived.

Now find out where your partner went on the days or during the periods shown and fill in a copy of the form below.

Note that you have to write **where** she or he went, as well as **how** (by what means of transport) and **at what time** she or he arrived there.

At the bottom of this page you'll see some phrases to help you with the **how** questions.

quand?	où?	par quel moyen de transport?	arrivée à...
hier soir			
lundi soir			
mardi matin			
mercredi soir			
jeudi matin			
vendredi soir			
samedi après-midi			
dimanche matin			
pendant les vacances de Pâques			
pendant les vacances de Noël			

 en voiture

 par le train

 en taxi

 dans le car

 en bateau

 à pied

Both you and your partner are looking at the six drawings below. The only difference is that the positions of the six drawings are different.

Your job is to try to be the first to work out where your partner's drawings are placed.

Take turns to ask each other about the drawings.

You need to ask, for example, about your partner's picture three *(image numéro trois)*: *Est-ce que le nez du monsieur est plus long que le nez de la dame?* Then continue to ask questions until you discover which of your pictures is like your partner's picture three.

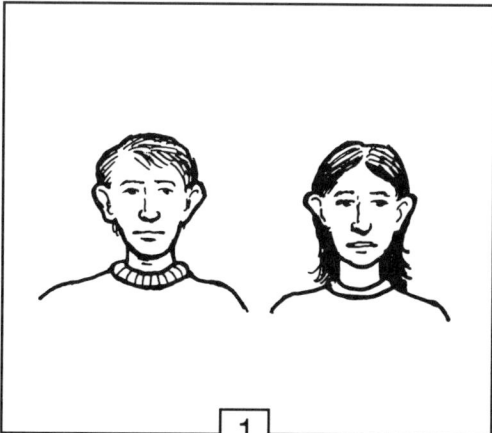

1

2

3

4

5

6

In this game, you and your partner will take it in turns to play the parts of the patient and doctor. For the first three interviews, you play the part of the doctor, and your partner is the patient.

Here are some technical details to help you to make your diagnosis in each case. Make your diagnosis and prescribe whatever you think is necessary. Your teacher will check your diagnosis to see how you have coped!

	symptômes	depuis…	diagnostique	remède
a	fièvre mal à la poitrine nausées	2–3 jours	bronchite	antibiotiques rester au chaud
b	mal au foie	1 jour	jaunisse	antibiotiques semaine au lit régime spécial
c	mal au bas ventre très fort; douleur sur le côté mal au coeur	une demi-heure	appendicite	à l'hôpital – vite
d	température élevée boutons les yeux qui pleurent	1 jour	rougeole (measles)	antibiotiques éviter la lumière rester au lit
e	mal à la gorge	2–3 jours	angine (tonsilitis)	antibiotiques 3 jours au lit

For the second set of three interviews, you are the patient and your partner will play the part of the doctor. For each interview, choose one of the sets of symptoms below and answer your partner's questions in line with them.

	symptômes	depuis…
1	mal au foie	1 jour
2	nez bouché éternuements brûlures de gorge	4 jours
3	mal au ventre très fort sur le côté nausées	une demi-heure

Expressions utiles

j'ai des nausées	I feel very sick
des douleurs fortes	strong pains
des brûlures de gorge	sore throat
des boutons	spots
j'ai les yeux qui pleurent	my eyes are running
mal au foie	pain in liver
je vais vous faire une ordonnance	I'm going to write you a prescription
vous devez aller…	you must go…
éviter la lumière	avoid the light
du sirop	medicine
rester au lit	stay in bed
prenez ces pilules	take these tablets
le bas ventre	lower abdomen

You and your partner will, in turn, play the parts of a TV interviewer and a star. To begin with, you are the interviewer.

Your job is to find out the following information about your star, *Jacques* (or *Marie*) *Célèbre:*

1 real name; family details (parents/brothers & sisters)
2 home (where is this?)
3 where does she/he work?
4 musical taste
5 taste in food
6 favourite drinks
7 what she or he has been doing recently?
8 what she or he is going to do in the near future?

Now you and your partner can swap roles.

Here are the details of your star's life to help you answer your partner's questions:

stage name	*Marie* (or *Marcel*) *Daudet*
real name	*Alphonse* (or *Alphonsine*) *Daudet*
home	Bordeaux
work address	Studio 45 à Paris
taste in music taste in food favourite drinks	} you choose
recently	played Hamlet in Shakespeare's play
soon	will play a part in a *'feuilleton'* (soap, TV series)

You and your partner will take it in turns to play the parts of a waiter and customer in a café in France.

For the first game, you are the customer.

In fact, you play the part of the only person in the group of tourists who speaks French, so you have to order for everyone at your table.

Each of the five people in your party wants something to eat and something to drink.

One person wants tea without milk, another wants a cheese sandwich. One of you orders a pâté sandwich... and is then convinced that the pâté has gone off *(le pâté n'est pas bon)*.

It's now your turn to play the part of the waiter. Below is a list of the drinks and snacks sold at the café, together with the prices:

boissons		snacks	
thé (nature)	14F	croque-monsieur	2F
thé (au citron)	13F 30	oeuf dur	5F
café	7F	sandwich au jambon	13F
café crème (grand)	7F 50	sandwich au fromage	14F
café crème (petit)	4F 50	sandwich au pâté	15F
Orangina	10F		
Coca-Cola	10F		
menthe à l'eau	16F		
bière à la pression	11F		
bière en bouteille	13F		

Bear in mind that:

1 Your heating system has failed so you are unable to serve any hot drinks.

2 You have strict instructions not to sell any alcoholic drinks to minors, so watch out for English tourists who may try it on.

Répertoire Français–Anglais

There is also an English–French list, beginning on page 178 which covers only those words which you need to know.

A

a	has (she/he/it)
à	to/at/in
abeille(l') *f*	bee
abri (l') *m*	shelter
accès aux quais (l') *m*	to the platforms
accueil (l') *m*	welcome/reception
acheter	to buy
actualités (les) *f*	news
actuellement	at the moment
addition (l') *f*	bill
affranchissements (les) *m*	stamps
agent des P et T (l') *m*	post office clerk
agneau (l') *m*	lamb
aider	to help
aimer	to like
aimerais	I would like
alcool (l') *m*	alcohol
Allemagne (l') *f*	Germany
allemand	German
aller et retour (un)	return ticket
aller simple (un)	single ticket
allez au/à la	go to the
alors	then/well
amande (l') *f*	almond
amène	brings (she/he)
amitiés (les) *f*	love (in letters)
s'amuser	to have fun
an (un)	a year
anglais	English
Angleterre (l') *f*	England
année (une)	a year
août	August
apprendre	to learn
après	after
arc (un)	arch/bow
argent (l') *m*	money
argenté	silver
arrivées	arrivals
arriver	to arrive
as (tu)	have (you)
ascenseur (l') *m*	lift
assez	enough/quite
assiette (l') *f*	plate/dish
atroce	awful
au revoir	goodbye
aussi	also
autorail (l') *m*	railcar
avec	with
avais	had (I/you)
avant	before
avant-hier	the day before yesterday
avez (vous)	have (you)
avoir	to have
avril	April

B

baba au rhum (le)	rum baba
babyfoot (le)	table football
baguette (la)	stick loaf
bain (le)	bath
balcon (le)	balcony (seat)
banane (la)	banana
banque (la)	bank
bâtiment (le)	building
beau	handsome /fine
beaucoup	a lot
beurre (le)	butter
bidon (le)	jerrycan
bien	good/well
bien sûr	of course
bientôt	soon
bière (la)	beer
bifteck (le)	steak
billet (le)	ticket
biscuit (le)	biscuit
blanc	white
blé (le)	wheat
blessure (la)	injury
bleu	blue
bocal (le)	jar
boire	to drink
bois (tu)	drink (you)
bois	wood
boisson (la)	drink
boit	drink (she/he)
boîte (la)	box/tin
bon/bonne	good
bonjour!	hello/good day
boucherie (la)	butcher's shop
boucherie chevaline (la)	horse butcher's
boulangerie (la)	bakery
bout (le)	end
bouteille (la)	bottle
boutique (la)	shop
bras (le)	arm
Bretagne (la)	Brittany
brosse (la)	brush
buffet (le)	buffet
bureau (le)	office
bus (le)	bus

C

ça	that
ça va?	how are you?
cachet (le)	tablet
caddie (le)	trolley
cadenas (le)	padlock
café (le)	coffee/café
cahier (le)	exercise book
caisse (la)	cash desk
camionnette (la)	van
camping (le)	camp site
canard (le)	duck
canif (le)	penknife
canne (la)	cane
capot (le)	bonnet
car (le)	bus

caravane (la)	caravan	combien	how much/many?
carie (la)	decayed tooth	comme	how/in the way of
carotte (la)	carrot	comme ci comme ça	so so
carré (le)	square	comment	how/what
cartable (le)	school bag	comment ça va	how are you
carte postale (la)	postcard	commissariat (le)	police station
casier (le)	pigeon-hole	complet	full up
cassé	broken	complet (le)	suit/full up
ce	this/that	composter	to stamp (a ticket)
cela	that	comprends	understand (I/you)
célébrer	to celebrate	compris	included
celle	the one	comptoir (le)	counter
celui	the one	confiserie (la)	sweet shop
certain	some	confiture (la)	jam
ces	these/those	connais	know (I/you)
c'est	it is	connaître	to know (by acquain-
c'est à dire	that is to say		tance)
chaîne (la)	channel (TV)	consigne (la)	left luggage
chaise (la)	chair	construit	constructed
chambre (la)	bedroom	continuez (vous)	continue (you)
champ (le)	field	contravention (la)	fine
champignon (le)	mushroom	copain (le)	friend (male)
chance (la)	luck	copine (la)	friend (female)
changer	to change	correspond	corresponds
chanteur (le)	singer (male)	côte (la)	rib
chanteuse (la)	singer (female)	cou (le)	neck
chapeau (le)	hat	couleur (la)	colour
chaque	each/every	cour (la)	playground/yard
charcuterie (la)	pork butcher's	couteau (le)	knife
chariot (le)	trolley	couvert (le)	place setting
chat (le)	cat	craie (la)	chalk
chaud	hot	crayon (le)	pencil
chaussette (la)	sock	crème (un)	white coffee
chaussez (vous chaus-		crêpe (la)	pancake
sez du combien?)	what size shoes do you	crevé	burst
	take?	croque-monsieur (le)	cheese, ham on toast
chemise (la)	shirt	croque-madame (le)	cheese, ham and egg
chèque (le)	cheque		on toast
cher/chère	dear (masculine/	cuir (le)	leather
	feminine)		
chercher	to look for	**D**	
cheval (le)	horse	d'accord	OK
chevreau (le)	kid (young goat)	dame (la)	lady
chez	at (someone's house,	dans	in
	shop etc.)	d'autres	other
chien (le)	dog	de	of/from
choisi	chosen	dé (le)	dice
chose (la)	thing	décapotable	convertible
choucroute (la)	pickled cabbage	décembre	December
ciel (le)	sky	décrivez (vous)	describe (you)
cinéma (le)	cinema	définitivement	once and for all
circulaire	circular	déjeuner (le)	lunch
ciseaux (les) **m**	scissors	demain	tomorrow
citron (le)	lemon	demander	to ask
citron pressé (le)	lemon juice	demi (le)	half (of beer)
clé (la)	key	dent (la)	tooth
clef (la)	key	départs (les) **m**	departures
clignotant (le)	indicator	dépliant (le)	brochure
clou (le)	nail	depuis	since/for
coeur (le)	heart	derrière	behind
colle (la)	glue	des	some
collectionner	to collect	descendez (vous)	go down (you)
collège (le)	secondary school	désolé	sorry (masculine)

désolée	sorry (feminine)	étaient	were (they)
dessin animé (le)	cartoon	était	was (she/he/it)
devant	in front of	étalage (l') *m*	stall
difficile	difficult	été (l') *m*	summer
dimanche	Sunday	êtes (vous)	are (you)
discothèque (la)	disco	étoile (l') *f*	star
disque (le)	record	étranger (l') *m*	foreigner
distraction (la)	entertainment	examiner	to examine
se dit	means	expliquer	to explain
dois	must (I/you)		
doit	must (she/he/it)	**F**	
donner	to give	fabriquer	to make
donner rendez-vous	to arrange to meet	faim (la)	hunger
doré	golden	faire	to do/to make
dormir	to sleep	faire parvenir	to send
dos (le)	back	famille (la)	family
douane (la)	customs	farine (la)	flour
douche (la)	shower	ferme (la)	farm
doux	mild	fermier (le)	farmer
droguerie (la)	household products	fermière (la)	farmer
	shop	feu (le)	fire/light
droite (la)	right	feuille (la)	sheet/leaf
du	of the/some	feuille de soins (la)	treatment sheet
dur	hard	feuilleton (le)	series/soap opera
		feux (les) *m*	traffic lights
E		février	February
eau (l') *f*	water	fièvre (la)	fever
école (l') *f*	school	fille (la)	girl
écouter	to listen to	film (le)	film
écrire	to write	film d'épouvante (le)	horror film
s'écrit	is written	film policier (le)	detective film
efficace	efficient	fleuve (le)	river
eh bien	well	flipper (le)	pinball machine
élève (l') *m or f*	pupil	fois (la)	time
elle	she	font	do/make (they)
elles	they	formulaire (le)	form
embrayage (l') *m*	clutch	fort	strong
émission (l') *f*	programme	frein (le)	brake
emplacement (l') *m*	tent space	frère (le)	brother
employé de banque (l')		froid	cold
m or f	bank clerk	fromage (le)	cheese
en	in (a country)	fruits de mer (les) *m*	seafood
enchanté	pleased to meet you	fumer	to smoke
encore	again/still		
enfant (l') *m or f*	child	**G**	
enlever	to remove	garage (le)	garage
ennuyeux	irritating/boring	garçon (le)	boy
énormément	enormously	gare (la)	station
entre	between	gare routière (la)	bus station
entrée (une)	starter dish	gâteau (le)	cake
environ	about/roughly	gauche (la)	left
épaule (l') *f*	shoulder	genou (le)	knee
épicerie (l') *f*	grocery	gentil	nice/kind
escalier (l') *m*	stairs	glace (la)	ice-cream/mirror
escargot (l') *m*	snail	gorge (la)	throat
espagnol	Spanish	grand	big
espère	hope (I/he/she/it)	gratult	free (of charge)
essence (l') *f*	petrol	grenadine (la)	pomegranate syrup
essuie-glace (l') *m*	windscreen wiper	grippe (la)	flu
essuyer	to wipe/to clean	gris	grey
est	is (she/he/it)	guêpe (la)	wasp
est-ce que	is it that	guerre (la)	war
et	and	guichet (le)	ticket office

H

habiter	to live
hâte (la)	haste
de hauteur	in height
heure (l') **f**	hour/time
hier	yesterday
homme (l') **m**	man
horloge (l') **f**	clock
hors série	exceptional/custom (car)
huile (l') **f**	oil

I

ici	here
il	he/it
ils	they
il y a	there is/there are
immatriculation (l') **f**	registration number
infirmière (l') **f**	nurse
informations (les) **f**	news
interdit	forbidden
intéressant	interesting

J

j'ai	I have
jambon (le)	ham
janvier	January
jaune	yellow
je/j'	I
jeu (le)	game
jeudi	Thursday
jeune	young
jouer	to play
jouet (le)	toy
jour (le)	day
journal (le)	newspaper
journaux (les) **m**	newspapers
juillet	July
juin	June
jupe (la)	skirt
jus (le)	juice

L

la	the
là-bas	over there
lac (le)	lake
laisser	to let/allow
lait (le)	milk
lame (la)	blade
lapin (le)	rabbit
large	wide
lavabo (le)	washroom
laver	to wash
le	the
léger	light
légume (le)	vegetable
lessive (la) **f**	washing powder
lettre (la)	letter
librairie (la)	bookshop
limonade (la)	lemonade
lire	to read
lis	read (I/you)
lit	read (he/she)

lit (le)	bed
livre (la)	pound
livre (le)	book
location (la)	accommodation to rent
loin de	far from
louer	to rent/hire
loup (le)	wolf
lourd	heavy
lui	to her/to him
lundi	Monday
lunettes (les) **f**	glasses

M

ma	my
maçon (le) **m**	builder
magasin (le)	shop
mai	May
maillot de corps (le)	vest
main (la)	hand
mairie (la)	town hall
mais	but
maïs (le)	maize
maison (la)	house
mal (le)	pain
malade	ill
manger	to eat
manteau (le)	coat
marché (le)	market
marcher	to walk
mardi	Tuesday
marron	brown
mars	March
marteau (le)	hammer
matière (la)	subject
matin (un)	morning
mauvais	bad
me	me/to me
ménagère (une)	housewife
menthe (la)	mint
mer (la)	sea
merci	thank you
mercredi	Wednesday
mère (une)	mother
mes	my
Messieurs	gentlemen
mesure (la)	measure
mets	put (I/you)
miauler	to miaow
mignon	nice
millefeuilles (le)	cream slice
miroir (un)	mirror
mis	put
mobylette (la)	moped
moi-même	myself
moins	less
mois (un)	month
mon	my
montez (vous)	go up (you)
montre (une)	watch
mordu	bitten
moustique (un)	mosquito
mur (un)	wall
musée (un)	museum

N

naissance (une)	birth
navet (un)	turnip (bad film)
ne...pas /n'...pas	not
noir	black
nom (un)	name
nombreux	numerous
non	no
nourriture (la)	food
nous	we
de nouveau	again
novembre	November
nuit (une)	night
numéro (un)	number

O

octobre	October
oeuf (un)	egg
on	we
ont	have (they)
or (l') **m**	gold
ordinaire	2-star petrol
ordinateur (l') **m**	computer
ordonnance (l') **f**	prescription
orge (l') **f**	barley
orientations (les) **f**	directions
ou	or
où	where
oui	yes
ouvre	opens
ouvreuse (une)	usherette

P

pain (un)	loaf/bread
pamplemousse (le)	grapefruit
panneau (le)	notice/roadsign
papeterie (la)	stationer's
papier (le)	paper
paquet (le)	parcel/pack
par	by/through
parapluie (un)	umbrella
parce que (qu')	because
pare-brise (le)	windscreen
parfois	sometimes
parler	to speak
à part	apart from
pas de panique	don't panic
pas mal	not bad
passager (un)	passenger
passeport (le)	passport
passer	to pass
passer	to be on (TV)
patiner	to skate
patinoire (la)	skating rink
pâtisserie (la)	cake shop
péniche (la)	barge
pense	thinks
père (le)	father
perdu	lost
permanence (la)	study lessons
permis (le)	driving licence
perroquet (le)	parrot
personne (la)	person

pèse	weighs (she/he/it)
pétillant	sparkling
petit déjeuner (le)	breakfast
petit four (le)	biscuit
petit pain (le)	bread roll
peut	can (she/he/it)
phare (le)	headlamp
pharmacie (la)	chemist's
à pied	on foot
pilote (un)	pilot
pilule (une)	pill
piqûre (une)	injection
piscine (la)	swimming pool
place (la)	square
plage (la)	beach
plan (le)	map
planche (la)	plank/board
plaque (une)	plate/bar/packet
plaque d'immatriculation	number plate
plat (un)	dish
plein air (le)	open air
plomber	to fill (a tooth)
plus	more
pneu (le)	tyre
poil (un)	hair
poire (une)	pear
poisson (le)	fish
pomme (la)	apple
pomme de terre (la)	potato
porc (le)	pork
portefeuille (le)	wallet
porter	to carry/to wear
poste (la)	post office
poule (la)	hen
poulet (le)	chicken
pour	for/in order to/to
pourpre	purple
pourquoi	why
pourrais	could (I)
pourriez (vous)	could (you)
posséder	to possess/own
préférer	to prefer
premier/première	first
prendre	to take
prendrai	will take (I)
prenez (vous)	take (you)
prénom (le)	first name
près	near
à la pression	draught (beer)
prêter	lend
prise	taken
prochain	next
producteur (un)	producer
produit ménager (un)	household product
professeur (un)	teacher
se promener	to go for a walk
puis	then

Q

quai (le)	platform
quand	when
quart (le)	quarter
quatorze	fourteen

quel	what/which	scie (la)	saw (tool)
quelle	what/which	secrétaire (un/une)	secretary
quelles	what/which	sel (le)	salt
quels	what/which	semaine (la)	week
qui	who/which	sens	feel
quincaillerie (la)	hardware store	septembre	September
		sera	will be (she/he/it)
R		serais	would be
radis (le)	radish	serpent (un)	snake
rail (le)	rail	sers	serve (I/you)
raisin (le)	grape	service (le)	service
rapide	fast	serviette (une)	briefcase
rapide (le)	express	ses	his/her
rayé	striped	si	if
rayon (le)	department	s'il vous plaît	please
regarder	to watch/to look at	sincèrement	yours sincerely
règle (la)	ruler	sirop (un)	syrup/medicine
religieuse (une)	cake (type of éclair)	slip (un)	pants
remplir	to fill	soeur (une)	sister
remplissez (vous)	fill (you)	soif (la)	thirst
rencontrer	to meet	soir (un)	evening
réparer	to repair	son	his/her
repas (un)	meal	sont venus	came (they)
répondre	to reply	sonner	to ring
réserver	to reserve	sorte (une)	sort/kind/type
rester	to stay/to remain	sortie (la)	exit
retourner	to return	sortie de secours (la)	emergency exit
rétroviseur (le)	rearview mirror	sortir	to go out
réunir	to gather together	sous-titré	sub-titled
réviser	to revise	sous-total (un)	sub-total
revoir	to see again	sous-vêtements (les) **m**	underclothes
rhume (un)	cold	souvent	often
richesse (la)	wealth	stade (un)	football ground
rideau (un)	curtain	stylo (le)	pen
rien	nothing	suite	continued
rive (la)	(river) bank	super (le)	3-4 star petrol
rivière (une)	river	sur	on
robe (la)	dress	sûr	sure
rond	round	surtout	above all
rosé	rosé (wine)	syndicat d'initiative (le)	tourist office
roue (une)	wheel		
rouge	red	**T**	
rouler	to drive/to go	table (la)	table
roulette (la)	drill (dentist's)	tableau (le)	board
routier (un)	lorry driver	taille (la)	size/waist
ruban (un)	ribbon	taon (le)	horse fly
		tasse (la)	cup
S		temps (le)	weather
sa	his/her	tente (la)	tent
sac (le)	bag	terrasse (la)	terrace (of café)
sacoche (une)	little bag	tête (la)	head
saignant	rare (steak)	thé (le)	tea
sais	know (I/you)	timbre (un)	stamp
salle (la)	room	toi	you
salle de bain (la)	bathroom	toilettes (les) **f**	toilets
salut!	hi! goodbye!	total (le)	total
samedi	Saturday	tour (la)	tower
sans	without	tour (le)	tour
sans doute	probably	tournevis (le)	screwdriver
sauce (une)	gravy/sauce	tournez (vous)	turn (you)
saucisse (la)	sausage	tous	all/every
savoir	to know (facts)	tout de suite	at once
savon (un)	soap	tout droit	straight ahead

toute	all	vestiaire (le)	cloakroom
travail (un)	work/job	vêtements (les) **m**	clothes
travailleur	to work	veut	wants (she/he/it)
travailleur (le)	worker	veux	want (I/you)
traverser	to cross	viande (la)	meat
traversez (vous)	cross (you)	victoire (la)	victory
très	very	vidéoclip (le)	pop video
trop	too	vie (la)	life
truffe (une)	truffle	viens	come (I/you)
truite (une)	trout	vient	come (she/he/it)
tu	you	vignette (la)	label
		ville (la)	town
U		vin (le)	wine
un	a	vinaigre (le)	vinegar
une	a	violon (le)	violin
utiliser	to use	vis (une)	screw
		voici	here is/here are
V		voie (une)	track
va	goes/is going (she/he/it)	voilà	there is/there are
vais	go/am going (I)	voir	to see
vaisseau (un)	vessel	voiture (une)	car
vaisselle (la)	washing up	vol (un)	flight/theft
vallée (la)	valley	voleur (un)	thief
variété (la)	variety	voudrais	would like (I/you)
vélo (le)	bicycle	voulez (vous)	want (you)
vélomoteur (le)	moped	voyez (vous)	see (you)
vend	sells (she/he/it)	vu	seen
vendredi	Friday		
vénéneux	poisonous		
verre (un)	glass	**Y**	
vert	green	y	there
veste (une)	jacket	y-a-t'il	is there/are there

Répertoire Anglais–Français

This word list only contains words which you should be familiar with.

A

a	*un/une*
adult	*un adulte*
after	*après*
again	*encore*
also	*aussi*
and	*et*
apple	*une pomme*
arm	*un bras*
arrivals	*(les) arrivées*
to ask	*demander*
at once	*tout de suite*
August	*août*

B

back	*le dos*
bad	*mauvais*
bag	*un sac*
bakery	*une boulangerie*
bank	*une banque*
bank employee	*un employé de banque*
beach	*une plage*
because	*parce que*
bedroom	*une chambre*
beer	*une bière*
before	*avant*
behind	*derrière*
between	*entre*
bicycle	*un vélo*
big	*grand*
biscuit	*un biscuit/un petit four*
black	*noir*
blue	*bleu*
book	*un livre*
boring	*ennuyeux/ennuyeuse*
bottle	*une bouteille*
boy	*un garçon*
bread	*le pain*
breakfast	*le petit déjeuner*
briefcase	*une serviette*
brochure	*une brochure/un dépliant*
broken	*cassé*
brother	*un frère*
brown	*marron*
builder	*un maçon*
building	*un bâtiment*
bus	*un autobus/car*
bus station	*la gare routière*
but	*mais*
butchers	*une boucherie*
butter	*le beurre*
to buy	*acheter*
by	*par*

C

cake	*un gâteau*
camp-site	*le camping*
car	*une voiture*
car-park	*le parking*
caravan	*une caravane*
to carry	*porter*
cash desk	*une caisse*
cassette	*une cassette*
cat	*un chat*
chair	*une chaise*
chalk	*une craie*
channel (TV)	*une chaîne*
cheese	*le fromage*
chemist	*une pharmacie*
cheque	*un chèque*
chicken	*un poulet*
class	*une classe*
clock	*une horloge*
clutch	*l'embrayage*
coat	*un manteau*
cold (a cold)	*un rhume*
cold	*froid*
to collect	*collectionner*
colour	*une couleur*
computer	*un ordinateur*
to cross (e.g. a road)	*traverser*
cup	*une tasse*
curtain	*un rideau*

D

to dance	*danser*
day	*un jour/une journée*
December	*décembre*
departures	*(les) départs*
difficult	*difficile*
disco	*la discothèque*
do	*faire*
dog	*le chien*
draught beer	*une bière à la pression*
dress	*une robe*
to drink	*boire*
to drive	*rouler*
duck	*un canard*

E

each	*chaque*
to eat	*manger*
egg	*un oeuf*
emergency exit	*la sortie de secours*
England	*Angleterre (l')*
enormously	*énormément*
entertainment	*une distraction*
every	*chaque*
excuse me	*excusez-moi*
exit	*la sortie*

F

family	*la famille*
far from	*loin de*
farm	*une ferme*
fast	*rapide/vite*
father	*un père*
February	*février*

fever	la fièvre
fill in	remplir
first	premier
fish	un poisson
flight	un vol
flour	la farine
flu	la grippe
food	la nourriture
foot	un pied
on foot	à pied
football ground	le stade
forbidden	interdit
fourteen	quatorze
free	gratuit
Friday	vendredi
fruit	un fruit

G

garage	un garage/une station service
gentleman	Monsieur
German	allemand
Germany	Allemagne (l')
girl	une fille
to give	donner
glass	un verre
glasses	des lunettes
golden	doré
to go	aller
to go (by car)	rouler
to go along	descendre
to go up	monter
good	bon/bien
goodbye	salut/au revoir
grape	du raisin
grapegruit	un pamplemousse
gravy	la sauce
green	vert
grey	gris
grocery	une épicerie
guitar	une guitare

H

hairdresser (male)	un coiffeur
hairdresser (female)	une coiffeuse
half (beer)	un demi
ham	le jambon
hammer	un marteau
hardware store	la quincaillerie
hat	un chapeau
he	il
head	la tête
heart	le coeur
heavy	lourd
hello	bonjour
hen	une poule
her/his	son/sa/ses
hotel	un hôtel
hour	une heure
house	une maison
housewife	une ménagère
how	comment
how are you	ça va?
how much/how many	combien?

I

I	je/j'
ice-cream	la glace
ice-rink	la patinoire
if	si
important	important
in	dans
in (a country)	en
in (a town)	à
interesting	intéressant
it	il/elle

J

jacket	une veste
jam	la confiture
January	janvier
juice	le jus
July	juillet
June	juin

K

key	la clé/la clef
kid (child)	un gosse
kind	gentil
knee	un genou

L

lady	une dame
lake	un lac
lamp	une lampe
left	la gauche
left luggage	une consigne
lemon juice	un citron pressé
letter	une lettre
lettuce	une salade
lift	un ascenseur
light	léger
like	comme
to listen to	écouter
to live	habiter
to look for	chercher
lorry driver	un routier
lost	perdu
lost property office	le bureau des objets trouvés
(a) lot of	beaucoup de

M

machine	une machine
main dish	le plat principal
to make	faire
man	un homme
map	un plan
March	mars
market	un marché
May	mai
to meet	rencontrer
mint	la menthe
mirror	la glace/le miroir
month	un mois
moped	le vélomoteur

mother	la mère		**R**	
motor	un moteur		rabbit	le lapin
mountain	une montagne		record	un disque
mouth	la bouche		red	rouge
my	mon/ma/mes		return ticket	un aller et retour
			right	droite
N			river	un fleuve/une rivière
name	un nom		river bank	une rive
neck	un cou		roll	un petit pain
news	les informations		room	une salle
newspaper	un journal		room (bedroom)	une chambre
no	non		roughly	environ
not	ne…pas		round	rond
not at all	pas du tout		Russia	la Russie
note (bank)	un billet (de banque)		Russian	russe
November	novembre			
nurse	une infirmière		**S**	
			salad	une salade
O			salt	le sel
October	octobre		Saturday	samedi
of	de		sausage	une saucisse
of course	bien sûr		school	une école
OK	OK/d'accord		school (secondary)	un collège
on	sur		scissors	des ciseaux
on (a bike)	à (bicyclette)		sea	la mer
on Monday	lundi		seat	une place
one	un (1)		secretary (m)	un secrétaire
open air (in the)	en plein air		secretary (f)	une secrétaire
other	d'autres		to see	voir
over there	là-bas		to send	envoyer
			September	septembre
P			she	elle
packet	un paquet		shirt	une chemise
pancake	une crêpe		shoe	une chaussure
panic (don't)	pas de panique		shop	une boutique
paper	un journal		shoulder	une épaule
passenger	un passager		silver	argenté
pear	une poire		singer (male)	un chanteur
pen	un stylo		singer (female)	une chanteuse
petrol	de l'essence (f)		single ticket	un aller simple
pill	une pilule		sister	une soeur
pilot	un pilote		skirt	une jupe
pink	rose		to skate	patiner
platform	un quai		skating rink	la patinoire
to play	jouer		sky	le ciel
playground	une cour		to sleep	dormir
policeman	un agent		to smoke	fumer
police station	le commissariat		so…so	comme ci comme ça
pool (swimming)	la piscine		soap	le savon
pork butchery	la charcuterie		sock	une chaussette
to possess	posséder		some	des
post office	la poste		some (particular things)	certains
potato	la pomme de terre		soon	bientôt
to prefer	préférer		soup	la soupe
prescription	une ordonnance		to speak	parler
problem	le problème		square (in town)	la place
programme	une émission		square (shape)	le carré
purple	pourpre		stairs	un escalier
			stamp	un timbre
Q			starter (dish)	une entrée
quarter	un quart		station	une gare
quite	assez		station *(métro)*	une station
			stationers	une papeterie

steak	un bifteck	**V**	
street	une rue	value	une valeur
striped	rayé	van	une camionnette
Sunday	dimanche	vegetable	des légumes
sweet shop	une confiserie	very	très
to swim	nager		
swimming pool	une piscine	**W**	
		to walk	marcher
T		wall	le mur
to take	prendre	wallet	le portefeuille
taxi	le taxi	washing powder	la lessive
tea	le thé	washing up	la vaisselle
teacher	le professeur	to watch	regarder
telephone	le téléphone	watch (wrist)	une montre
to telephone	téléphoner	water	de l'eau (f)
television	la télévision	we	on
tent	une tente	to wear	wear
thank you	merci	Wednesday	mercredi
the	le/la/les/l'	what	quel/quelle
theatre	le théâtre		quelles/quels
then	puis	when	quand
there	y	where	où
there are/there is	il y a	which	quel/quelle
there you are	voilà		quelles/quels
these	ces	which	qui
they	ils/elles		
thief	le voleur	white	blanc
those	ces	who	qui
Thursday	jeudi	why	pourquoi
tip	un pourboire	wide	large
to (a town)	à	windscreen	le pare-brise
toilets	des toilettes	wine	le vin
tomorrow	demain	with	avec
too (as well)	aussi	wood	le bois
too (much/many)	trop de	wound	la blessure
tooth	une dent		
tourist office	le syndicat d'initiative	**Y**	
tower	une tour	yellow	jaune
town	une ville	yes	oui
town hall	une mairie	yesterday	hier
traffic lights	les feux	yoghurt	le yaourt
track	une voie	you (friendly)	tu
truffle	une truffe	you (formal)	vous
Tuesday	mardi	young	jeune
turkey	une dinde	your (friendly)	ton/ta/tes
turn	tournez	your (formal)	votre/vos
U			
umbrella	un parapluie		
to use	utiliser